World Health Organization
Regional Office for Europe
Copenhagen

Treatment approaches to alcohol problems

by

Nick Heather

Centre for Alcohol and Drug Studies,
Northern Regional Alcohol and Drug Service,
Newcastle City Health NHS Trust,
Newcastle-upon-Tyne, United Kingdom

WHO Regional Publications, European Series, No. 65

Text editing by Mary Stewart Burgher

WHO Library Cataloguing in Publication Data

Heather, Nick
Treatment approaches to alcohol problems / by Nick Heather

(WHO regional publications. European series ; No. 65

1.Alcohol drinking 2.Alcoholism - prevention & control - therapy
3.Europe I.Title II.Series

ISBN 92 890 1329 X (NLM Classification: WM 274)
ISSN 0378-2255

The Regional Office for Europe of the World Health Organization welcomes requests for permission to reproduce or translate its publications, in part or in full. Applications and enquiries should be addressed to the Office of Publications, WHO Regional Office for Europe, Scherfigsvej 8, DK-2100 Copenhagen Ø, Denmark, which will be glad to provide the latest information on any changes made to the text, plans for new editions, and reprints and translations already available.

PRINTED IN FINLAND

Acknowledgements

The author is extremely grateful to the following colleagues who gave valuable advice and comments on earlier drafts of some chapters of this book: Alison Conway, Eilish Gilvarry, Stephen McCarthy and Duncan Raistrick.

Contents

Introduction

This book is intended for planners, managers and providers of treatment for alcohol-related problems at the national, regional and local levels in the Member States of the WHO European Region. It provides an overview of effective approaches to treatment currently in use, the methods associated with these approaches and the available research evidence for their effectiveness and cost–effectiveness in eliminating or reducing alcohol problems.

The book covers issues related to target client groups, goals, settings and staffing of different treatment approaches, as well as broader considerations of underlying treatment philosophy and theoretical foundations. It also addresses the role of coercion in treatment. It concludes with a model for a comprehensive treatment service and how such a service might be established.

In this book, treatment has a wide-ranging meaning. It includes intervention by non-specialist personnel in community settings, as well as that by specialists in clinics and other agencies focusing on alcohol-related problems. The types of intervention that are usually referred to as counselling are also included. In addition, the mutual aid organized and facilitated by self-help groups such as Alcoholics Anonymous is seen as a form of treatment. Thus, the personnel responsible for delivering treatment in this broadly defined sense include members of a range of professions – such as medicine, nursing, clinical psychology, occupational therapy, social work and probation – as well as trained alcohol counsellors without formal qualifications, voluntary helpers and so-called recovering alcoholics. All these groups can play a part in the national treatment response to alcohol problems.

Treatment also includes detoxification, although this is better viewed as a prelude to treatment or counselling and detoxification alone can rarely achieve a lasting change in drinking behaviour. Further, a chapter addresses assessment, which is regarded as an essential component of any adequate treatment service. The treatment of medical conditions that are the consequences of excessive drinking, including organic brain syndromes and psychiatric disorders, is not included.

This overview of treatment is based entirely on publications in English. This means that the literature reviews, research reports and commentaries mentioned emanate mainly, although not entirely, from English-speaking countries. The reader must ultimately judge the extent to which this literature is relevant to the experience of other cultures.

There is no presumption that the English-speaking countries in question have all the answers on treating alcohol problems, since this is manifestly far from true. What this book offers is a distillation of a particular experience and tradition in responding to individual alcohol problems that must be assessed on its merits. Nevertheless, if theory, research and practice in the field of alcohol problems are seen as forms of scientific activity, the relevant body of scientific knowledge should be capable in principle of international application.

SOURCES

The preparation of the book benefited greatly from the thorough reviews of treatment effectiveness in the field of alcohol problems that have been made in the last decade or so *(1–6)*. In addition, people from a range of professional disciplines have written several practical guides to the conduct of treatment *(7–14)*, conveying the results of varied clinical experience. These have provided useful source material for the book, and the reader is encouraged to consult the original works for a fuller account of the issues covered.

TERMINOLOGY

A word on terminology is necessary before proceeding. The recipients of treatment for alcohol problems are referred to here as clients rather than patients (except where the context is obviously medical, as in detoxification services). This is because of the broadening of the professional groupings involved in treatment, which has led to a certain demedicalization of the treatment response, and because the word patient implies too passive a role for the recipient of treatment in the effort to change drinking behaviour. There is now consensus that successful treatment must involve the active participation, commitment and skills of the problem drinker. (A similar logic could be used to argue that the more general term intervention should replace the word treatment, but this seems too clumsy.) These terminological niceties, however, in no way imply any attempt to downgrade the crucial role of the medical profession in the treatment of problem drinkers.

The preceding paragraph suggests that the terms alcoholism and alcoholics have given way to the terms problem drinking and problem drinkers. This derives from a view of alcohol problems that rejects the idea of a qualitative break between the most serious forms of alcohol problem, previously and conventionally known as alcoholism, and those of a less serious variety. Both alcohol-related problems and alcohol dependence are seen as lying on a continuum ranging from mild to severe *(15)*. One consequence of this is that problem drinking, as used in this book, does not refer to alcohol problems of a less serious nature than those usually described by alcoholism. Rather, problem drinking carries the all-embracing sense of "repetitive use of beverage alcohol causing physical, psychological or social harm to the drinker or to others" *(16)*. Nevertheless, if the reader is unfamiliar with this change in terminology or not persuaded of its usefulness, this should not detract from the book's aims. A person who prefers the alcoholism concept can easily understand the descriptions of treatment and reviews of effectiveness contained here.

EFFECTIVE AND INEFFECTIVE TREATMENT

As mentioned, this book focuses on effective treatment for alcohol problems. This means that most of the treatment approaches and methods described here have been judged to be effective from the results of controlled trials meeting conventional standards for scientific rigour. While the extent of scientific support varies among these methods, it would normally be expected that effectiveness had been demonstrated in more than one trial.

The book also includes treatment methods that may not have been definitely shown to be effective, but show promise of effectiveness. The chief criterion for regarding a method as promising is that it is coherently linked to a wider body of theory, research and practice; in other words, there are rational and empirical grounds for believing the method might be effective. Some of the new pharmacological agents described in Chapter 9 come into this category, as does the cue exposure approach described in Chapter 10. A promising method may also have been found to be effective in other fields where behaviour change is the aim and it is reasonable to predict a transfer of effectiveness to alcohol problems. This is the case with cue exposure.

The ineffective methods that have been largely omitted are of two quite different kinds. First, some methods used on alcohol problems have been convincingly shown to be ineffective, in the sense that they have produced treatment outcome results inferior to those of other methods in controlled trials. The list of such methods is long and includes videotape self-confrontation and other confrontational methods, non-specific counselling, educational lectures and films, group psychotherapy, individual insight psychotherapy, antianxiety medication, psychedelic drugs and residential/milieu treatment *(4)*. Although the world of treating alcohol problems is largely irrational in nature, at least some of these methods – such as videotape self-confrontation and psychedelic drugs – have been virtually abandoned, one hopes, as a consequence of scientific evidence.

The other kind of ineffective treatment method comprises those that have not been shown to be effective or ineffective because they have not been subjected to adequate research evaluation. More accurately, these methods are described as unsupported by research. By far the most outstanding example here is the Fellowship of Alcoholics Anonymous (AA). Although some controlled research has been conducted on AA, with generally disappointing results, none of this represents a fair test of AA's effectiveness in comparison with other methods among the people for whom it appears best suited. Nevertheless, AA can be described as effective in another important sense: it has proved immensely popular among problem drinkers. In any event, no book on the treatment of alcohol problems could afford to ignore AA. Its role in the range of services on offer to problem drinkers comprises the main topic of Chapter 12.

The irrationality of the world of treating alcohol problems is starkly demonstrated by the fact that treatment methods shown to be effective are little used, while the methods commonly used are typically unsupported by scientific evidence *(1)*. This is especially true in the United States but applies to a varying extent in other countries. The point is important enough to bear repeating: the treatment methods most commonly used to treat alcohol problems – group psychotherapy, individual insight psychotherapy, educational lectures and films, residential milieu therapy – receive no justification from scientific evidence. More encouragingly, however, there are signs that some effective methods, chiefly the cognitive–behavioural methods covered in Chapters 10 and 11 and the motivational interviewing techniques described in Chapter 8, are beginning to be more widely used in some countries.

One might think it no accident that the most effective treatment methods are also the ones that are best founded on neurophysiological or psychological theories. Moreover, these effective treatments are on the whole more cost-effective than those it is recommended that they replace. A crucial aim of this book is to increase the use of effective and cost-effective treatment methods in Europe.

1

Targets of Treatment: Broadening the Base

The most significant development in the treatment of alcohol problems in recent years has been a broadening of the base to include client groups who would not previously have been considered to be suitable targets of intervention *(3)*. This widening of treatment activity has embraced the large group of drinkers whose problems are less severe than those traditionally termed alcoholics, who have high levels of dependence on alcohol. It has also included drinkers who show no obvious alcohol-related problems but are at risk of developing them. Many of these new targets for intervention do not complain of or seek help for an alcohol problem. They must therefore be screened and identified in the community, and persuaded that they should reduce or eliminate their alcohol consumption.

There are several justifications for the extension of treatment activity. The first and most obvious is the need to intervene early, before problems have produced permanent damage to the drinker's health and welfare, and before dependence has reached a level that makes successful treatment more difficult. Although some treatment methods have been shown to be more effective than others, and conventional treatment as a whole can be shown to produce economic benefits for the health care system (see Chapter 13), it must be conceded that the results of treatment for severely affected problem drinkers are poor in absolute terms. In addition, the assumption of an inexorable worsening of alcohol problems, if treatment is not received, is unfounded; many problem drinkers recover on their own without expert help, and others move into and out of problem status at various times during their lives *(16,17)*. Nevertheless, sufficient numbers of problem drinkers show a progressive deterioration to justify the inclusion of early intervention and the secondary prevention of more serious problems as a component of any national treatment response. Apart from the obvious humanitarian grounds for this approach, early intervention can be expected to save resources by preventing chronic illness and the need for protracted and expensive treatment in later years.

Early intervention, however, is not the only justification for the widening of the net. The harm done to a society through alcoholic beverages can easily be demonstrated to extend far beyond that associated with severely dependent people. For many types of problem (such as accidents, violence and the loss of industrial productivity), the major contribution to alcohol's costs to society comes from drinkers with less frequent and less serious problems. This results from the way alcohol consumption is distributed in a population and the much greater number of people at the lower end of the spectrum of alcohol consumption and related problems. As to the primary prevention of alcohol problems, this has been dubbed "the preventive paradox" *(18)*: the best way of reducing the aggregate of alcohol-related problems in a society is to focus on curtailing the drinking of moderate rather than heavy drinkers. The same logic can be applied to treatment: to reduce the total harm caused by alcohol to society, it is better to focus on the large number of people with relatively mild problems than the much smaller number with very serious problems. This new imperative is clearly consistent with a public health approach to alcohol-related harm and with other measures designed to reduce the harmful effects of alcohol on society *(19)*.

This should not be taken to suggest, however, that people with serious problems should be ignored. On humanitarian grounds alone, adequate treatment services for the severely dependent must continue to be made available. Thus, the recommendation is not to change the focus of attention and the allocation of resources but to extend them; the increased expenditure involved will prove cost-beneficial to society in the long run.

NOMENCLATURE AND CLASSIFICATION

Nomenclature proposed in a WHO memorandum issued in 1981 *(20)* is still useful in expressing this new view of alcohol problems in society. In place of the unsatisfactory terms drug abuse and drug misuse, the memorandum suggests the following:

(a) *Unsanctioned use.* Use of a drug that is not approved by a society or a group within that society...;

(b) *Hazardous use.* Use of a drug that will probably lead to harmful consequences for the user – either to dysfunction or to harm ...;

(c) *Dysfunctional use.* Use of a drug that is leading to impaired psychological or social functioning ...;

(d) *Harmful use.* Use of a drug that is known to have caused tissue damage or mental illness in the particular person.

The last three categories have proved useful concepts for a clearer understanding of alcohol problems. In particular, hazardous and harmful use can be defined in terms of drinking limits recommended by medical and other authorities in each country: limits that may be periodically reviewed in the light of the latest scientific evidence. Such limits also provide essential foundations for brief, community-based interventions. A useful term for describing all three categories (hazardous, harmful and dysfunctional use of alcohol) is excessive drinking.

DEFINING ALCOHOL DEPENDENCE

Alcohol dependence can be operationally defined by the elements of the alcohol dependence syndrome *(21),* currently the most popular model of dependence in professional and scientific circles. In this view, dependence should not be regarded as an either/or phenomenon but as lying on a continuum of severity running through the population of problem drinkers. (Indeed, all heavy and regular drinkers are likely to have some degree of dependence as recorded by well established measuring instruments – see Chapter 3.) Thus, it is profitable to speak of problem drinkers, not as being dependent as opposed to non-dependent, but as having low (or mild), moderate and high (or severe) levels of dependence.

In addition, the WHO memorandum *(20)* recommended that the distinction between physical and psychological dependence be abandoned. The two were inextricable and no clear and useful separation could be made. A less misleading term for physical dependence was neuroadaptation. The memorandum argues that dependence manifests as a behavioural pattern and should be seen as a "psycho-physiological-social syndrome" in which it is difficult or impossible to separate the physical and psychological aspects *(20)*. It also emphasized the important distinction between alcohol dependence and alcohol-related disabilities. These were correlated but conceptually independent phenomena; it was possible to be highly dependent on alcohol but with little or no disability, and vice versa.

OTHER CRITERIA

The idea of an alcohol dependence syndrome has been incorporated into the fourth edition of the *Diagnostic and statistical manual* (DSM-IV) of the American Psychiatric Association *(22)*. While the present writer has considerable reservations about this conceptual scheme, it is widely used and classification in this area should be standardized and replicable. It is included for the benefit of readers who wish to make diagnoses of alcohol dependence in a manner intended to be reliable and objective.

DSM-IV establishes criteria for the diagnosis of substance dependence and substance abuse. The criteria for substance dependence *(22)* are:

> A maladaptive pattern of substance use, leading to clinically significant impairment or distress, as manifested by three (or more) of the following, occurring at any time in the same 12-month period:
>
> (1) tolerance, as defined by either of the following:
>
> (a) a need for markedly increased amounts of the substance to achieve intoxication or desired effect
>
> (b) markedly diminished effect with continued use of the same amount of the substance
>
> (2) withdrawal, as manifested by either of the following:

(a) the characteristic withdrawal syndrome for the substance ...

(b) the same (or closely related) substance is taken to relieve or avoid withdrawal symptoms

(3) the substance is often taken in larger amounts or over a longer period than was intended

(4) a persistent desire or unsuccessful efforts to cut down or control substance use

(5) a great deal of time is spent in activities necessary to obtain the substance ..., use the substance ..., or recover from its effects

(6) important social, occupational or recreational activities given up or reduced because of substance use

(7) continued substance use despite knowledge of having had a persistent or recurrent physical or psychological problem that is likely to have been caused or exacerbated by the substance ...

Specify if:

With physiological dependence: evidence of tolerance or withdrawal (i.e. either item (1) or (2) is present).

Without physiological dependence: no evidence of tolerance or withdrawal (i.e. neither item (1) nor (2) is present).

The criteria for substance abuse are:

A. A maladaptive pattern of substance use leading to clinically significant impairment or distress, as manifested by one or more of the following, occurring at any time during a twelve month period:

(1) recurrent substance use resulting in a failure to fulfil major role obligations at work, school, or home ...

(2) recurrent substance use in situations in which it is physically hazardous ...

(3) recurrent substance-related legal problems ...

(4) continued substance use despite having persistent or recurrent social or interpersonal problems caused or exacerbated by the effects of the substance ...

B. The symptoms have never met the criteria for Substance Dependence for this class of substance

DSM-IV also provides a set of course specifiers (remission criteria), as well as criteria for a range of alcohol-induced disorders (intoxication, withdrawal, persisting dementia, persisting amnestic disorder, psychotic disorder, mood disorders, anxiety disorder, sexual dysfunction and sleep disorder). The proper use of DSM-IV requires specialized clinical training. These diagnostic criteria are, of course, subject to periodic revision as knowledge increases.

The *ICD-10 Classification of mental and behavioural disorders (23)* provides another diagnostic scheme. For those familiar with this system, it gives F10 as the overall code for "disorders due to use of alcohol". Four character codes include acute intoxication, harmful use, dependence syndrome, withdrawal states, psychotic disorder, amnesic syndrome, residual and late-onset psychotic disorder, and other and unspecified mental and behavioural disorders.

SPECIAL POPULATIONS

Despite the usefulness of overarching concepts such as hazardous or harmful use and alcohol dependence, alcohol problems appear in a remarkable diversity of forms *(3)*. One way partly to capture this diversity is to consider the special population groups that can show alcohol problems. Any discussion of targets of treatment must include these groups because it is essential to ensure that treatment services are provided for them.

Special populations include the various racial and ethnic minority groups that may be found in each country. The expression of alcohol problems may take unique forms among such people and the treatment offered should reflect this. Age is another important source of classification, and both young and elderly problem drinkers have particular kinds of difficulty. Gender is another important distinction, and women in particular have special kinds of alcohol problem that have tended to be neglected in the past.

Another way of defining special populations is by their functional characteristics *(3)*: their social, clinical or legal status. Such groups include people convicted of drink-driving offences, those with a dual diagnosis in which a psychiatric disorder is combined with alcohol dependence or problems, prisoners and homeless people with alcohol problems, and the families of problem drinkers, particularly their children.

Chapter 15 discusses arrangements for accommodating the needs of special populations in a comprehensive treatment service.

2

Detoxification

Among the groups identified as targets of treatment in the preceding chapter were problem drinkers with varying levels of neuroadaptation to alcohol. A withdrawal syndrome is likely to follow the cessation of drinking by a person who is neuroadapted. Detoxification is the process whereby a patient recovers from alcohol intoxication under supervision so as to minimize the severity of withdrawal symptoms. These symptoms include hyperthermia, tachycardia, increased respiration rate, hypertension, nausea and vomiting, tremor, sweating, agitation and anxiety; in severe cases, disorientation, tactile, auditory and visual hallucinations, and convulsions may occur.

For many problem drinkers the alcohol withdrawal syndrome is not especially uncomfortable or dangerous. For the minority that experiences delirium tremens (DTs), seizures or both (1–3% of problem drinkers *(3)*, depending on the levels of consumption among the population in question), however, withdrawal can be life-threatening. Safety is therefore of paramount importance in the provision of detoxification services.

Nevertheless, compared with treatment to change drinking behaviour, detoxification is a straightforward matter. Detoxification is conventionally seen as requiring a stay in hospital and the use of medication to reduce withdrawal symptoms. Recently, however, alternative approaches to inpatient, medicated detoxification have been developed that are suitable for the majority of problem drinkers. These are community-based, medicated detoxification and inpatient, non-medicated detoxification.

COMMUNITY-BASED DETOXIFICATION

Community-based detoxification is suitable for patients showing or likely to show a mild-to-moderate withdrawal syndrome. Those with any of the following characteristics should be excluded from community-based detoxification, and detoxified at a specialist inpatient unit:

(*a*) current severe withdrawal (severe tremor, tachycardia above 110 beats per minute, fits, DTs, clouding of consciousness or hallucinations) at the time of assessment;

(*b*) a history of severe withdrawal, such as DTs or seizures;

(*c*) the expectation of imminent severe withdrawal, for example, following extremely heavy consumption;

(*d*) illnesses, such as a chest infection, pneumonia or pancreatitis, that require immediate treatment (DTs being more common when such illnesses are present);

(*e*) polydrug use with heavy intake of other drugs in addition to alcohol; and

(*f*) evidence of suicidal ideation or severe depressive disorder.

Community-based services can be divided into outpatient detoxification and home detoxification. The former can be done either at a specialist treatment unit or at various suitable locations in the local community, such as general practice health centres. For those needing somewhat more help with detoxification or other pressing difficulties, day patient facilities can be used. Outpatient or day patient services are recommended for the great majority of people in need of alcohol detoxification.

Alterman et al. *(24)* have described outpatient detoxification as used in the United States. They report that it can be just as safe and effective as inpatient care, while being much more accessible to patients and providing easier links with continuing treatment. Its chief advantage, of course, is that it is much cheaper than inpatient detoxification.

Although home detoxification is also cheaper than inpatient detoxification, it is considerably more expensive than the outpatient variety and is recommended only for patients who have difficulty travelling to outpatient facilities, for example, because they live in a remote area or because of disability or child care problems. The model of home detoxification developed by Stockwell et al. *(25)* involves a psychiatric nurse who supervises the administration of anxiolytic medication and provides support to the patient and members of the family. During the period of detoxification, the nurse visits the patient's home on at least a daily basis, monitors the severity of withdrawal by a special scale, breathalyses the patient to check on abstinence and administers the next dose of medication. A nominated general medical practitioner should be available to supervise the detoxification and assist in case of medical emergency.

Successful home detoxification also requires supportive and sensible relatives or friends to stay with the patient during the period of detoxification, monitor the administration of medication and call for medical assistance if necessary. The patient must not have ready access to a supply of alcohol or other drugs at home. If the home environment is unsuitable for detoxification for these reasons, inpatient detoxification should be chosen. Stockwell *(26)* gives further details of a home detoxification programme.

In addition to being more cost-effective than inpatient, medicated detoxification, community-based detoxification is more accessible and acceptable to drinkers. Indeed, many of those undergoing outpatient or home detoxification not only prefer it but would refuse to accept hospital admission, mainly because of the associated stigma.

Nevertheless community-based detoxification has some disadvantages. First, it is likely to yield lower success rates than inpatient detoxification. This is partly because of the greater accessibility and the wider range of drinkers reached, and partly because the cues and temptations associated with heavy drinking cannot be entirely removed in the natural environment. Also, as stated above, community-based detoxification is not appropriate for those who are likely to experience a severe withdrawal syndrome.

NON-MEDICATED INPATIENT DETOXIFICATION

The other alternative to conventional detoxification is to use inpatient facilities, but not medication. Like community-based detoxification, this is suitable for people undergoing a mild-to-moderate withdrawal with no concomitant medical problems. It can be used, for example, where conditions are not conducive to home detoxification or where no outpatient detoxification service exists. The main advantage of non-medicated detoxification is that it is considerably cheaper than the medicated variety in terms of drugs and staff. Also, this approach avoids the risks of dual dependence and side effects.

Non-medicated detoxification is based on the simple principle that supportive counselling in a quiet, non-threatening environment can prevent or reduce withdrawal symptoms, even relatively serious symptoms such as hallucinations. Staff need not be health professionals, but lay people who have received special training in techniques to alleviate withdrawal symptoms, maintain the drinker's reality base and deal effectively with potentially violent episodes. The only exception to the non-medicated nature of this regime is that thiamine should be given as a preventive measure against Wernicke's encephalopathy and Korsakoff's syndrome.

Sparadeo et al. *(27)* describe a "social-setting detoxification program" developed in Canada. This programme emphasizes referral to long-term treatment proper as one of its major outcome criteria. Experience at units for non-medicated detoxification in Sydney, Australia shows that only 2.5% of patients per year need to be transferred to a general hospital for medical management. Mattick & Jarvis give guidelines for non-medicated management *(5)*.

MEDICATED INPATIENT DETOXIFICATION

Inpatient medicated detoxification is indicated when withdrawal is severe. Its practical basis is that a dose of a sedative drug should be matched to the patient's severity of withdrawal.

The drugs most often used in detoxification are the benzodiazepines diazepam (Valium) and chlordiazepoxide (Librium), and chlormethiazole (Heminevrin), a compound structurally related to thiamine. Diazepam and chlormethiazole have the advantage for use in detoxification of being anticonvulsants. Chlormethiazole should not be used in home detoxification because of a significant risk of respiratory depression when mixed with alcohol; it also has a high dependence potential and should not therefore be used in outpatient detoxification. Medical practitioners should familiarize themselves with these drugs and acquire experience with matching dosage and duration against severity of withdrawal. Edwards *(7)* and Saunders *(28)* give guidelines to pharmacological intervention in detoxification.

MONITORING WITHDRAWAL

No matter the kind of detoxification used, all patients in withdrawal or at risk of developing a withdrawal state should, whenever possible, be regularly monitored according to a recognized scale of withdrawal severity. This will help staff decide when to call for medical input and help the clinician make decisions on such issues as the commencement or adjustment of medication, and transfer to other facilities. More generally, it will ensure that standardized and objective criteria are used during the detoxification process. One such scale is the clinical institute assessment for withdrawal from alcohol *(29)*.

EFFECTIVENESS AND COST–EFFECTIVENESS

As to the effectiveness of home detoxification, Stockwell et al. *(25)* assess the value of a new programme by a variety of outcomes. They conclude that home detoxification with supervised medication is as effective and safe, among the patients for whom it is suitable, as inpatient care. Hayashida et al. *(30)* compared the effectiveness and costs of inpatient and outpatient detoxification for problem drinkers with mild-to-moderate withdrawal symptoms. They found no differences in effectiveness between the two, but the inpatient programme was over ten times more expensive. Similarly, for so-called social-setting detoxification, Sparadeo et al. *(27)* reported that costs per patient were about 15% of those for inpatient medicated detoxification. A great deal of other evidence has accumulated to suggest that both outpatient medicated and inpatient non-medicated withdrawal are effective, safe and cheap alternatives to hospital detoxification for suitable patients.

A RANGE OF DETOXIFICATION FACILITIES

The comments about the high cost–effectiveness of community-based detoxification should not be taken to mean that inpatient facilities should be closed down. Nor should the advantages of non-medicated detoxification be interpreted as a recommendation to abandon the use of drugs. As already emphasized, inpatient medicated detoxification is essential for the small minority of problem drinkers likely to experience severe withdrawal, if the risk of death is to be avoided. Purpose-built facilities are preferable to beds on acute medical or psychiatric wards because the latter are liable to be noisy, distracting and threatening environments, making withdrawal more difficult and distressing for the patient.

What is needed for an effective and efficient detoxification service is a range of facilities – outpatient/home, non-medicated and medicated – that can meet the needs of patients with different home circumstances and levels of withdrawal. In addition, although agreement to undergo further treatment or counselling should never be made a condition of offering detoxification, withdrawal that is not followed by some further attempt to alter drinking behaviour is unlikely to have much lasting effect. Edwards *(7)* provides a useful general discussion of and guide to detoxification.

3

Assessment

Problem drinkers vary in the kinds of alcohol problem they show and in the kinds of people they are. It is therefore unlikely that they will all respond successfully to the same type of treatment programme, and the main aim of assessment is to determine what kind of programme is most likely to help each client. If a service offered only one kind of treatment to all its clients, there would be little need for assessment beyond the requirements of record keeping. For a modern and efficient treatment service, however, in which a range of modalities should be available, assessment is an essential preparation for treatment.

Assessment serves five formal purposes:

1. to familiarize the therapist thoroughly with the nature of a particular client's alcohol problem;
2. to describe the precise nature of the problem and the client's specific characteristics, strengths and weaknesses, so that an appropriate and individualized intervention can be planned;
3. to provide a basis for the measurement of progress in meeting treatment goals;
4. to enable the overall efficiency of the service to be monitored; and
5. to allow the relative success of different treatment methods to be evaluated.

Assessment also serves the more informal purpose of allowing the development of a rapport between therapist and client without which treatment is unlikely to succeed. This is a two-way process – a matter of the client getting to know the therapist as much as of the therapist getting to know the client. If the therapist approaches the client at first contact with courtesy, respect and empathy, mutual trust can be established and any defensiveness in the client reduced. This in turn encourages the client to begin taking a fresh perspective on the nature of the problem. In this sense, a good assessment is the first step in the treatment process.

TIME AND OTHER RESOURCES

The length and thoroughness of an assessment varies across treatment settings, depending on the degree of specialization in alcohol problems of the agency in question, the time and personnel available and other factors. If a service has only a few treatment options on offer, the volume of assessment should be reduced to reflect this restricted range; there is no point in collecting information for its own sake. Data gathering is an expensive process and should not be used prodigally.

This much having been established, the importance of assessment should be made clear *(7)*. Staff should not regard it as a tedious chore that merely delays the commencement of the real work of treatment. It is difficult to exaggerate the potential value of a process designed to reach a thorough understanding of a person's problems in the overall context of his or her life, with the object of developing a treatment plan that stands the best chance of being helpful. In addition, many agencies may devote unnecessary staff time to the intervention proper, time that could be reallocated to more efficient assessment. This may save the agency time and money in the long run through more cost-effective treatment.

Assessment can be streamlined, however, to reduce costs. First, as suggested by the Institute of Medicine *(3)* in the United States, a brief initial screening can be used to identify those clients who do not have an alcohol problem or whose problem is sufficiently minor that they can benefit from a minimal intervention (at least, as a first option). Chapter 7 discusses screening in conjunction with opportunistic brief interventions, but here it may merely be pointed out that a treatment agency can use similar instruments, such as AUDIT *(31)*, for this screening purpose. This obviates the need for further, lengthy assessment in some cases.

The Institute of Medicine report *(3)* also recommends the use of short screening at subsequent stages in the assessment procedure. This and the streamlining of assessment by means of self-completion instruments are covered later in this chapter.

One sort of investment in assessment is unavoidable. This is the need for treatment staff to constantly review their skills and current knowledge of assessment methods, and to seek to redress deficiencies where necessary. The importance of such an attitude is highlighted by evidence that good assessment considerably increases the rate of entry into treatment *(32)*.

TYPES OF ASSESSMENT

One should not confuse assessment with the act of filling in forms and questionnaires; it is much more than this. The temptation to regard a battery of questionnaires as an adequate substitute for the personal contact that the client needs and probably expects on approaching a treatment agency should be avoided. Certainly, someone who has decided to seek help, for whatever reason, is disheartened to receive a large pile of blank forms for completion rather than the opportunity to talk to another human being.

On the other hand, the accurate quantification of aspects of the client's problem and other features of the case by means of valid and reliable measuring instruments is an indispensable part of the assessment process for several reasons. First, notes taken in a face-to-face interview are sure to be imperfect: the interviewer may overlook important features of the case or express them in such a summarized manner as to have little meaning for anyone else. When the client presents again for treatment at some time in the future, as unfortunately is often the case, the interviewer's written impressions usually convey a less accurate picture of the client's status than a score on a widely used measuring instrument whose properties are well known. The latter assists an understanding of the way the problem has evolved over time. In short, quantified assessment provides a means of communication between therapists of possibly different professional backgrounds at different points in time. (Of course, staff may extend this communication to the client by explaining, as far as possible, the purpose of the instrument in question and the significance of the scores.)

Second, face-to-face interviewing is expensive in terms of staff time and training. Moreover, not all staff can be assumed to possess the necessary skills and those who do should have received proper training in interviewing techniques and empathic listening. Thus, the use of instruments completed by clients can make considerable savings.

Finally, the main advantage of standardized, quantified assessment is, of course, that it is objective. Judgements based on personal interviews must always have an element of subjectivity, no matter how skilled or experienced the interviewers, and there is no guarantee that clients are assessed in the same way by different interviewers. On the other hand, if an instrument possesses high validity and reliability, as it should, its use can ensure that the assessment is not influenced by the vagaries of time, place and the personal philosophy of the assessor. The use of standardized measuring instruments, based on normative data, places the client's characteristics in an accurate relationship with those of other clients and the normal population, thus putting the problem in its proper perspective.

Nevertheless, some unique, subtle and possibly crucial features of the presentation of a problem are not amenable to quantification. Information gained from a sensitively conducted personal interview must therefore supplement even the most sophisticated measurement approach. An efficient and flexible assessment package might contain a judicious mixture of three types of procedure:

- personal interview
- self-administered pencil-and-paper tests
- computerized self-assessment.

In addition to the aim of establishing a good rapport with the client, a personal interview should be mainly concerned with taking the client's history, preferably by the person who is to be the therapist or counsellor. Edwards *(7)* provides a useful framework and guidelines for taking a comprehensive history from problem drinkers. If the exercise is to achieve its object of providing a fully rounded narrative history of the client's drinking and general life circumstances up to the point of presentation, the interview must be structured. Leaving the contents and direction to the individual interviewer, however experienced, involves too great a risk of serious omission and idiosyncratic recording. In addition, interviews should cover clients' reasons for seeking help, their perception of the problem, their needs, specific requests, expectations of treatment, and other important matters *(7)*.

As stated above, self-administered pencil-and-paper tests can provide much of the information needed for a thorough assessment. Clients should preferably complete such tests after contact has been made in a personal interview, and the need for such an assessment should be carefully explained. Staff usually need to provide only minimal supervision, give simple instructions, answer questions and check that forms have been satisfactorily completed. Obviously, clients with a sight or hearing impairment and those with poor reading skills need more face-to-face interaction.

The modern alternative to pencil-and-paper tests is an interactive computer program with the same contents as a questionnaire battery. Some clients may feel this is too impersonal an approach to information gathering and resent it, but their number is likely to decrease as popular experience of working with computers grows. There is evidence that this form of assessment gives equivalent, if not better results for the same contents as pencil-and-paper tests and face-to-face interviews *(33)*. While expensive to establish, such a system may well pay dividends in the long run through increased efficiency. It is also ideally suited to the requirements of monitoring and evaluating treatment.

ASSESSMENT DOMAINS

This section does not provide an exhaustive review of all the possible areas that might be covered in an assessment of alcohol problems or list all the measuring instruments that might usefully be included. Rather, it briefly describes the most obvious categories and suggests a few instruments where appropriate. This does not mean, however, that instruments not mentioned here are of no value. The National Institute on Alcohol Abuse and Alcoholism in the United States produced a handbook *(34)* attempting to describe all known (English-language) assessment instruments used in treating alcohol problems in 1985; an update is shortly to appear.

The Institute of Medicine *(3)* recommended that assessment be sequential and divided into problem assessment and personal assessment. This seems a useful scheme. The following assumes that clients have already passed through a short screening procedure that has weeded out those without an alcohol problem and those who are suitable for minimal intervention, such as brief advice and a self-help manual.

Problem Assessment

Problem assessment refers to matters directly related to the client's use of alcohol and may be divided into the following domains.

Alcohol Consumption

Information on the level, frequency and patterning of the client's current alcohol consumption is indispensable and must be carefully gathered. The traditional way of doing this, the so-called quantity–frequency (QF) method, asks clients to estimate the average frequency of drinking occasions and the amount typically consumed per occasion. This method *(35)* has been shown to be highly inaccurate, and should be abandoned except for rough screening. Much preferable is a detailed retrospective diary of actual drinking over a given period – say, the previous week or, if that was untypical, the last typical week in the recent past – using prompts of time, place and drinking companions to elicit accurate recall. The most thorough and sophisticated procedure is the time-line follow-back method *(36)*, which uses a calendar to give detailed information on drinking over an extended period. This may be too time-consuming for many agencies' requirements.

Different indices of consumption, such as average level, intensity of drinking (that is, the amount consumed per typical occasion) and maximum estimated blood alcohol concentration, can be calculated from sufficiently detailed data. If a self-contained assessment package is used, such as the comprehensive drinker profile *(37)*, rules are given for calculating relevant variables and for classifying clients by drinking pattern, such as episodic (bout) or steady. While standardized instruments are recommended here, the assessor should be alert to the possibility of unusual or unique circumstances connected with alcohol use.

The client's past drinking is usually covered as part of the history taking, but should be recorded in the same fashion as current drinking to facilitate direct comparison. The lifetime drinking history *(38)* is a more formal method of obtaining such information.

Where the necessary facilities exist, the client's self-reports of drinking can be checked against biochemical and other laboratory measures of recent alcohol consumption *(39)*. At their present stage of development, however, these laboratory measures have been shown to be less efficient at estimating consumption than properly elicited self-reports. They should therefore not be used as alternatives to self-reports but only as corroborative evidence of validity. (This situation may change.) Another method of corroboration is to ask the spouse, partner or other person with intimate knowledge of the client's drinking, but this is no guarantee of accuracy.

This point in the assessment is also a convenient time to enquire about polydrug use, since in many countries a large proportion of clients use and may have problems with other drugs. A profile of use of all common psychoactive substances, including tobacco, should be obtained.

Alcohol Dependence

The assessment of alcohol dependence is essential and, of all the domains considered here, this is the one where the advantages of standardized measurement are probably greatest. This is because of the theoretical importance of the concept of dependence in the characterization of an alcohol problem and the potential value of its measurement in planning treatment *(7)*. Three well known instruments have various advantages and disadvantages *(40)*, and at least one of these should be used. They are the severity of alcohol dependence questionnaire *(41,42)*, the alcohol dependence scale *(43)* and the short-form alcohol dependence data questionnaire *(44)*. The last-named is less frequently used than the other two but is particularly sensitive to early signs of dependence.

Alcohol-related Problems

The assessment of alcohol-related problems should cover the whole range of negative consequences that might have been experienced by the client, including medical, psychological, financial, legal, vocational, social, marital and other problems. Many earlier instruments purporting to measure problems in fact confused alcohol-related problems and dependence. A relatively new instrument, the alcohol problems questionnaire *(45)*, is a pure measure of problems.

Motivation to Change

Recognition is growing of the importance of assessing clients' motivation to change their drinking behaviour. An understanding of the client's level of motivation is essential for effective counselling and may well determine the kind of therapeutic approach offered (see Chapter 8). The assessment can use an instrument – such as the University of Rhode Island change assessment *(46)*, based on Prochaska & DiClemente's model of stages of change *(47)* – or can simply be derived from the client's responses to appropriate questions. A new version of the readiness to change questionnaire *(48)*, which is specifically for populations seeking treatment, is under development.

Cognitive–behavioural Assessment

A detailed picture of the antecedents and consequences of alcohol use and of the client's craving for alcohol is useful, especially if a cognitive–behavioural approach to treatment (see Chapter 10) is to be adopted. This domain of assessment relies as much on skilled and systematic inquiry by the interviewer as on established questionnaires. The topics covered include the cues (the environmental or social situations, and positive or negative mood states) regularly associated with heavy drinking; the inventory of drinking situations *(49)* is useful here. The particular reinforcements gained from drinking (such as reduction of anxiety, membership of drinking group, increase in social confidence and reduction of shyness with the opposite sex) should also be ascertained. In addition to the reinforcements apparent to the interviewer, the client's expectations of reinforcement from drinking should be determined, using one of several instruments available for measuring expectations of outcome. Finally, the client's feelings of efficacy in coping with specific high-risk situations without relapse can be investigated with the situational confidence questionnaire *(50)*, and the strengths and weaknesses of the client's repertoire of coping skills can be examined with tools such as the situational competency test *(51)*.

Personal Assessment

Personal assessment concerns domains that are not necessarily associated with alcohol use. The Institute of Medicine *(3)* points out, however, that the problem and personal assessment may often overlap, because alcohol use may well affect more general areas of adjustment. For example, heavy drinking may have affected the client's occupational prospects, but it will be important to understand the general situation in this area, whether or not it has been affected by alcohol.

The Institute of Medicine *(3)* also suggests that, for many domains of personal assessment, a short screening exercise can be carried out to ascertain whether a problem exists. If so, more intensive assessment can be carried out to discover the exact dimensions of the problem in question; if not, further screening is not necessary and valuable time and effort can be saved.

While the list is by no means exhaustive, the following are the more prominent domains of personal assessment:

- sociodemographic factors
- physical health status
- psychiatric disorders
- cognitive functioning

- family relationships
- social functioning
- personality.

It is clearly essential to have accurate data on the client's age, marital status, employment status, socioeconomic level and educational attainments. In addition, it is obviously necessary to know about the client's medical history, current illnesses and symptoms, and use of medication. The client may have received a physical examination in conjunction with the referral; if not, one should be arranged. Of course, particular attention should be paid to the organic sequelae of excessive drinking.

It is important to know whether the client suffers from a concomitant affective or behavioural disorder (such as depression, phobic states or morbid jealousy). Depending on the nature and severity of such a disorder, referral onwards may be needed. At the very least, the identification of psychiatric disorders has important implications for the planning and conduct of treatment and for the client's prognosis. Screening here could be done with the general health questionnaire *(52)*, with more intensive and specific assessment if necessary.

Some indication of the client's general level of intellectual ability, as well as knowledge of any more specific impairments, may be useful in carrying out counselling. This is particularly important in view of the cognitive impairment that can be produced by prolonged heavy drinking. Many sorts of treatment require clients to be able to process abstract information, and any impairment to this or other higher intellectual functions should be known. The testing of cognitive functioning can affect the selection of treatment in several ways *(53)*. This is a domain that might well benefit from preliminary screening.

Assessment of the client's family relationships may be relevant in a number of ways. The interaction between the client and family members may have exacerbated the problem by somehow reinforcing heavy drinking; if so, it would be important to know this. In any case, the client's drinking is likely to have affected relationships within the family, and the role of family members in urging the client to seek help is an especially relevant piece of information. If an approach to treatment that involves the client's family or spouse is being considered (see Chapter 10), it must be based on a thorough assessment of the intimate relationships involved.

Social stability is an important predictor of successful response to treatment, and social functioning in general is an important aspect of treatment outcome. Several scales measure aspects of social functioning *(54)*. Under this heading, one may include specific areas such as occupational adjustment, criminal activity and legal problems. Finally, an indication of the client's personality, as assessed by the very large number of available tests, may be useful for certain purposes.

TIMING OF ASSESSMENT

So far, assessment has been discussed in the sense of a preparation for treatment – in other words, pretreatment assessment. The importance of assessment, however, extends beyond this stage.

In a sense, assessment is a continuing process that should extend throughout the treatment programme and beyond. The client's progress should be reviewed from time to time, particularly when decisions have to be made, such as whether to reduce the number of sessions or move on to a new phase of the programme. Specific assessment can be undertaken at these times, but information could already be available to underpin these decisions. For example, at the commencement of treatment the client could be asked to keep a regular record of the occurrence and circumstances of drinking, temptations to drink, particular difficulties experienced and so on.

Assessment should also be undertaken when the treatment programme proper is considered to have come to an end. Post-treatment assessment can be used to establish a record of the client's progress in various areas and the degree of success of the programme in meeting specified goals (see Chapter 5) – in other words, to monitor progress and the effectiveness of the programme for the client.

Assessment is also essential, of course, at follow-up. It is needed partly to evaluate the programme but also to check on the client's status following treatment, to determine whether he or she needs further help in the form of booster sessions, full re-entry into treatment or a different type of approach (see Chapter 11). Follow-up assessment is best conducted either at six months or one year following termination of treatment; the latter is likely to detect more stable outcomes, but less attrition is likely to be seen at six months. To achieve satisfactorily high follow-up rates, reliance on clients attending routine appointments at the clinic is unlikely to be sufficient. If resources permit, more active follow-up in the community, using trace contacts previously elicited from the client, is usually necessary.

In post-treatment and follow-up assessment, forms identical to or parallel with those used in pretreatment assessment should be employed whenever possible, to enable direct comparisons and meaningful estimates of change to be made. It is also essential to cover the same time period as before. Some fresh variables can be measured at follow-up, such as the client's overall satisfaction with the treatment given, the elements of the programme found especially useful and so on. Finally, some attempt should be made to capture the client's post-treatment living situation and how this affects drinking status, since there is evidence that this has an important impact on outcome (see Chapter 11).

VALIDITY OF CLIENT SELF-REPORTS

The truthfulness and accuracy of oral reports of drinking behaviour and alcohol problems by the clients of treatment programmes has long been a contentious issue. While concern about the validity of these self-reports is understandable, the issue has often been unhelpfully put. Self-reports are neither valid nor invalid in themselves; their validity depends on how the information is obtained. The characteristics of the client are not the only determinant of the accuracy of self-reports; the characteristics of the interviewer, the interview situation and the entire treatment setting are also highly pertinent. O'Farrell & Maisto *(55)* listed the conditions that were likely to favour either valid or invalid self-reports (Table 1).

Table 1. Conditions affecting the validity of client self-reports of drinking behaviour and alcohol problems

Conditions conducive to invalid self-reports	Conditions conducive to valid self-reports
Client has positive blood alcohol concentration at time of assessment.	Client is free of alcohol (or drugs) at assessment.
Client is experiencing withdrawal symptoms or acute physical/mental distress.	Client is stable, showing no major symptoms.
Unstructured, general or vague items are used in taking the drinking history.	Structured, carefully developed measures of drinking and related behaviour are used in taking drinking history.
Client is not aware that self-reports will be checked against objective criteria.	Client is aware that self-reports will be checked with other sources (laboratory tests, collateral sources, records).
Client receives minimal contact or supportive counselling.	Good rapport has been established with client.
Client shows poor compliance with the treatment regime.	Client complies with other aspects of treatment.
Client has clear motives to dissimulate (e.g. abstinence being a condition of parole or continued employment).	Client has no obvious reason for distorting reports of alcohol use.
Client doubts the confidentiality of information provided.	Client is assured of confidentiality of information.
Settings and procedures encourage clients to report certain types of behaviour (e.g. abstinence, limited drinking) and not others (e.g. heavy drinking).	Setting and procedures promote honest reporting.

Source: O'Farrell & Maisto *(55)*. Reproduced by kind permission of Elsevier Science Ltd, The Boulevard, Langford Lane, Kidlington, OX5 1GB, United Kingdom.

As well as trying to create conditions favourable to valid self-reports, one can check their accuracy against other sources of data. For example, clients who are intoxicated at the time of interview are liable to underestimate their consumption and problems but it is not always easy to judge from simple observation whether the client has been drinking. As a simple precaution, therefore, a breathalyser can be used, provided it can be done in such a way as not to impair the trust that has been established between client and therapist.

A check on reports of long-term drinking is to take blood for the measurement of mean corpuscular volume, and gamma-glutamyl-transferase and other liver enzymes. Holt et al. *(56)* summarize the advantages and disadvantages of the laboratory markers. Collateral sources of information – such as spouses, other close relatives, friends, and workmates – can be used in an attempt to corroborate self-reports, but their knowledge of the client's drinking is bound to be incomplete. Depending on the nature of the self-report in question, checks can be made with official records, although this usually requires the client's permission. Thus, all these sources of data are imperfect; at present, none can replace verbal self-reports or provide a single judgement of self-report validity. In this situation, the only solution is to use as many sources of information as possible in an approach known as convergent validity *(57)*.

MONITORING, EVALUATION AND RESEARCH

This section considers the last two purposes of assessment given at the beginning of the chapter: monitoring the efficiency of the treatment service and evaluating the success of different methods.

Discovering the effective and ineffective ingredients of the treatment service, so that improvements can be made, requires a thorough and comprehensive description of the client population as a first step. The particular kinds of problem and other characteristics of prognostic significance identified in this way can be compared with published data on other populations. With good follow-up data, the overall success rates of particular components of the service can be investigated and, probably more important, an attempt can be made to match the characteristics of clients with the success or failure of the treatment component in question (see Chapter 4). Other matters, such as initial attendance rate, treatment drop-out and aspects of compliance should also be monitored and ways of improving them tested.

This kind of activity can be subsumed under the general heading of clinical audit. Its importance is likely to grow as the principle of accountability in treatment provision gains acceptance.

The last, but by no means least significant, function of assessment is its contribution through research to an understanding of alcohol problems and their treatment. In addition to research projects that the treatment service itself may undertake – whether in the form of randomized clinical trials or quasi-experimental designs – it is not too fanciful to envisage a national treatment database to which most of the treatment agencies in a country would contribute *(3)*. Given sufficient common ground in the assessment systems used in different agencies, such a database could provide an invaluable means of analysing data on the relative effectiveness of different treatment methods and on relationships between outcome and client and treatment characteristics.

4

Treatment Matching

As established in the previous chapter, no single treatment approach is likely to be effective for all problem drinkers. Some evidence shows that the cognitive–behavioural approach is superior to others overall (see Chapter 10), but many exceptions are sure to be found when individual response to treatment is considered. Moreover, many methods come under the heading cognitive–behavioural and here, too, no single method can benefit every client.

The obvious solution is to seek a treatment method or approach that is especially suited to the individual client: in current jargon, to match clients to treatments. This is hardly a new or revolutionary principle. The idea has a long history in the literature on treating alcohol problems *(3)* and is commonplace in many areas of medical treatment.

Nevertheless, the notion of treatment matching has attracted a good deal of attention in the field of alcohol problems over the last 15 years, and fairly extensive literature has been devoted to it *(58–63)*. This is due mainly to a general recognition that the results of treatment, particularly of more severe alcohol problems, are relatively poor. The failure to match clients appropriately to optimal treatments may have contributed to the negative or inconsistent results of many studies of treatment outcome *(60)*, and skilful matching could produce a significant improvement in success rates *(61–63)*.

EVIDENCE FOR MATCHING

To illustrate the types of matching that have been studied, it is useful to describe some of the research that has been taken as evidence in its favour. Comprehensive reviews of the relevant evidence, which is complex and of several different kinds, are found elsewhere *(3,6, 60–63)*. Moreover, the issue of matching arises at various places throughout this book. This section provides only a few, well known illustrations of the matching principle.

Annis & Chan *(64)* compared the effects of a highly confrontational type of group therapy with those of no treatment among prisoners with alcohol problems. The results showed that clients who had high levels of self-esteem did better in terms of reconviction rates, than subjects given no treatment, while those with low self-esteem did worse. This study thus demonstrates the importance of using a matching variable – in this case, self-esteem – to decide who should receive a particular form of treatment. Clients with low self-esteem are not merely liable to show no benefit from confrontational group therapy, they are likely to be harmed by it. Had the authors not measured self-esteem and analysed their results accordingly, they would have found no difference in outcome between the treatment group and controls and might have concluded that treatment was completely ineffective.

McLelland et al. *(65)* discovered a different sort of matching relationship when they measured the degree of psychological disturbance or "psychiatric severity" among clients of a range of treatment programmes. They found that clients with high psychiatric severity did poorly with both outpatient and inpatient regimes, while those low on psychiatric severity did well regardless of treatment setting. Only in the middle range of psychiatric severity (about 60% of clients) was the outcome from different types of treatment linked to client characteristics. This demonstrates the crucial relationship between psychiatric severity and treatment outcome.

Finally, Kadden et al. *(66)* compared training in coping skills (see Chapter 10) with group therapy in a randomized controlled trial. The results showed that clients with higher sociopathy and psychopathology and lower cognitive impairment fared better with the training.

An unexpected finding was that clients with relatively greater cognitive impairment did better with group therapy, which the authors try to explain by proposing that coping skills training placed too many demands on the reduced learning abilities of those with significant cognitive impairment. This study suggests that it be routine to look for matching contingencies, both predicted and not predicted, in treatment outcome research data.

This should not be taken to mean, however, that matching in practice should be restricted to procedures for which there is hard research evidence. Most clinicians probably have pet theories, based on clinical experience and common sense, about which types of client are likely to respond best to which types of treatment. Provided that such guidelines are explicitly described and rational, there is no reason why they should not be implemented as matching procedures, at least on a trial basis. It is essential, however, that their effects be carefully evaluated.

WHAT TO MATCH

If asked, the staff of many treatment centres would probably say that they already do treatment matching. All this often means, however, is that they have a selective policy on client admission to the programme and then make some adjustments to a basic treatment regime, usually in terms of additional or ancillary services, depending on individual clients' characteristics. This should not be regarded as treatment matching. Rather, the term should be reserved for agency policies that allocate different clients to fundamentally different types of treatment according to some predetermined and explicit set of rules *(3)*.

Matching might be based on several factors. Matching on the basis of the client's personality or other general characteristics has already been mentioned *(64)*. Equally straightforward is matching according to the particular kinds of problem shown by clients: either problems related to or in addition to alcohol consumption. For example, those showing a high level of anxiety might receive anxiety management training; those lacking in social skills might be directed to social skills training; those with particular marital difficulties related to drinking might be offered marital therapy, and so on. This kind of matching principle formed the basis of the so-called "broad spectrum approach" to behavioural treatment *(67)* that became popular during the 1970s (see Chapter 10). Other candidates for matching variables are the client's level of alcohol dependence, degree of alcohol-related problems, age, gender and marital status.

In addition to the characteristics of the client, the characteristics of the therapist might be included in the matching equation. Certain therapists may do better with particular types of client. A straightforward example would be a female therapist for female clients. McLachlan *(68)* describes allocation to different therapists according to the client's "conceptual level" (degree of preference for simple as opposed to complex rules, and dependence on or independence from authority). The potential of self-matching, in which clients decide for themselves what type of treatment is optimal, is discussed later in this chapter.

There is also the question of what the client should be matched to. The discussion so far has focused on the type of treatment approach or method to be used. Irrespective of treatment type, however, matching can be made to the length of treatment (brief or intensive), the setting of treatment (such as inpatient or outpatient) and drinking goal (abstinence or moderation). Subsequent chapters address all these possibilities.

HOW TO CARRY OUT MATCHING

Miller *(62)* gives guidelines for the rational matching of individual clients with interventions, and the Institute of Medicine *(3)* discusses this topic at some length.

In the development of matching systems, the treatment methods should be fully and explicitly described in writing. This makes it easier to decide when referral to a particular treatment is appropriate, and helps to ensure that clients actually receive what they are intended to receive.

The rules linking the characteristics of clients to forms of treatment should also be clear and unambiguous: for example, the exact cut-off on a measuring instrument that indicates the need for treatment A rather than treatment B. More ambitiously, rules on matching can be organized into a complete system from which the preferred treatment method for every client entering the programme can be deduced. An example of such a system is the core shell treatment programme developed at the Addiction Research Foundation in Toronto, Canada *(3)*. On a somewhat smaller scale, Lindstrom *(63)* has provided a model for differential treatment selection; this is shown for illustrative purposes in Table 2. The model uses different combinations of four variables (psychiatric severity, social instability, need for structure and severity of dependence) to allocate clients to seven different treatment regimes.

Table 2. A model for differential treatment selection

Optimal client–treatment match	Psychiatric severity	Social instability	Need for structure	Severity of dependence
P I. Relapse prevention, controlled drinking	Low	Low/ Middle	Low	Low
P II. Relapse prevention, abstinence	Low	Low/ Middle	Low	High
P III. Outpatient treatment, less structured	Middle	Low/ Middle	Low	High
P IV. Outpatient treatment, highly structured	Middle	Low/ Middle	High	High
P V. Inpatient treatment, less structured	Middle	High	Low	High
P VI. Inpatient treatment, highly structured	Middle	High	High	High
P VII. Sheltered living environment	High	High	High	High

Source: Lindstrom *(63)*. Reproduced by permission of Oxford University Press.

Ambitious matching systems of this kind, however, are complex to administer and relatively costly to run. Whether this expense is justified in the interests of improved overall treatment outcomes must be a matter of judgement and the results of experience with such systems.

SELF-MATCHING

One kind of matching procedure is simple and inexpensive: allowing clients to choose the form of treatment they receive. This naturally assumes that clients receive accurate and objective descriptions of the available options in a form they can understand. Complete self-selection (the so-called cafeteria plan) has been recommended *(69)*, but self-matching can be confined to a limited range of appropriate options.

Miller *(62)* discusses the merits of self-matching. First, self-matching takes place in the real world; clients tend to seek out a form of treatment that they feel will benefit them, and are unlikely to enter or comply with a treatment method that does not make sense to them. Given that this kind of informal self-matching occurs, one would be sensible to take advantage of the fact and try to improve its effects.

Second, research on human motivation shows in general that people are more likely to carry through a course of action that they have chosen for themselves than one that has been chosen for them. At the very least, this ability to choose makes clients more likely to comply with and complete the treatment regime, and this in turn leads to superior outcome. There is evidence that clients allowed to choose their treatment among alternatives do better than those who have not been allowed to choose *(70)*.

A third and related point is that therapists often encounter resistance to treatment and denial of alcohol problems from clients. As argued in Chapter 8, resistance and denial are not so much properties of clients as characteristics of the interaction between clients and therapists. For this reason, clients are less resistant to treatment and more likely to acknowledge their problems if they have chosen their treatment themselves and therefore feel some responsibility for their progress towards recovery.

An objection to self-matching is that clients tend to choose the method that seems most attractive or seems to demand the least effort from them, rather than the one that is most likely to solve their problem. The validity of this objection must be a matter for research and experience with self-matching.

Even if self-matching as such is thought inadvisable, the therapist should negotiate the type of treatment with the client and apply it with his or her full knowledge and consent. Methods that are imposed without the client's understanding or agreement are unlikely to achieve their objectives.

PROJECT MATCH

Several very important questions concerning treatment matching may be answered by a research project that is under way in the United States, funded by the National Institute on Alcohol Abuse and Alcoholism and known as Project MATCH (Matching Alcoholism Treatment to Client Heterogeneity). The project is a five-year controlled study involving 8 treatment centres and 1600 subjects, and costing about US $30 million. It is undoubtedly the largest study ever mounted in the field of alcohol problem treatment, and so large a project may never be funded again.

It will study three treatment modalities: a twelve-step approach following the principles of AA and founded on the idea that alcoholism is a spiritual and medical disease (see Chapter 12); a cognitive–behavioural approach based on social learning theory (see Chapter 10); and a motivation enhancement approach, which is a less intensive form of therapy based on the principles of motivational psychology (see Chapter 8). Trained therapists will deliver each of these modalities during a twelve-week period. Clients will be recruited either from outpatients or from people eligible for aftercare following a standard residential programme, and will be randomly allocated to one of the three treatment modalities. By the inclusion of suitable measuring instruments, specific hypotheses will be tested regarding the types of client who benefit most from each treatment approach. Other matching relationships not predicted by the investigators will also be sought in the outcome data. In addition to a general test of the hypothesis that matching can improve overall treatment outcome, and the possible discovery of useful matching contingencies, the project will allow crucial comparisons between the main effects of the treatment modalities under study. The results of Project MATCH are eagerly awaited and should be available some time in 1996.

5

Treatment Goals

In an important sense, the treatment of alcohol problems has only one goal: to improve the client's overall quality of life. This may sound obvious and trivial, but is easily forgotten in an undue preoccupation with drinking behaviour. Thus, one implication is that the therapist must bear in mind other areas besides the client's drinking when planning treatment and evaluating its effects. Making gains in other areas is difficult, however, if excessive drinking is not eliminated or at least much curtailed. For this reason, the nature of the drinking goal selected for each client – whether total abstinence, harm-free drinking or some other outcome – usually forms the subject of discussions of treatment goals.

RANGE OF TREATMENT OBJECTIVES

First, however, we must consider the range of goals or objectives that can come into play when planning treatment in the individual case. The work of Mansell Pattison during the 1960s and 1970s was influential in alerting the field to the need to consider other areas of adjustment than drinking behaviour. Pattison et al. *(71)* discussed the following: physical health, psychological adjustment (or mental health), vocational adjustment and interpersonal relationships. The last category could usefully be broken down into social adjustment, in the wider sense of affiliation to social groups and living arrangements, and interpersonal adjustment, as defined by the quality of intimate relationships and the number of close friendships. There could also be a case for including a separate category of legal status and criminal activity. Since Pattison et al. wrote, polydrug use has exploded and this should be considered a separate category of adjustment, in addition to drinking behaviour. Finally, the risk of contracting HIV through injecting drug use and unsafe sexual behaviour could be relevant to many people whose alcohol consumption is their primary problem.

Chapter 3 implies that all these areas should be assessed and the client's progress determined in relation to these wider outcome criteria. The point here, however, is that they should not only be assessed but, where appropriate, be incorporated in the treatment plan as specific goals of treatment. This is because degrees of adjustment and improvements in these areas are not necessarily highly correlated with each other; they are relatively independent areas of functioning. They also show only modest correlations with drinking behaviour. For example, a person may become a successful abstainer but still show poor psychological adjustment; on the other hand, heavy drinking may still be present to some extent but noticeable improvements may occur in social or occupational adjustment. Depending on the client's life situation and particular problems, drinking goals should be supplemented by specific targets in other areas of general adjustment.

DRINKING GOALS: ABSTINENCE VERSUS MODERATION

Should problem drinkers always be directed to total and lifelong abstinence, or can some of them responsibly be advised to attempt a reduction in drinking to harm-free levels? This has been one of the most controversial topics in the field over the last 20–30 years. More recently, it has become less contentious owing to the emergence of a consensus on how these two treatment goals should be used. The moderation goal has become far more acceptable in the United Kingdom, Australia and some other countries than in the United States, but even the latter shows signs of greater acceptance of its use in some circumstances.

The Evidence

The evidence shows, first, that some people who have been classified as problem drinkers or alcoholics can successfully return to controlled, harm-free drinking and maintain this pattern of drinking over an extended period of time. Heather & Robertson *(72)* reviewed a great deal of evidence to support this assertion in 1983, and the number of studies in its favour has substantially increased since then. Second, there appears to be no upper limit to the severity of the problem that absolutely precludes the possibility of resumed control; the phenomenon has occasionally been noted in the most chronic and deteriorated of cases.

Third, however, resumed normal drinking becomes less likely as the level of dependence and/or problems increases *(73)*; at the highest level of dependence it is a relatively rare event (Fig. 1). (The fact that moderation is extremely difficult for the highly dependent individual does not necessarily mean that problem drinking is best seen as an irreversible disease; the drinker's difficulties can also be explained in conditioning and other learning theory terms.)

Fig. 1. Relationship between level of alcohol dependence and the likelihood of successful controlled drinking

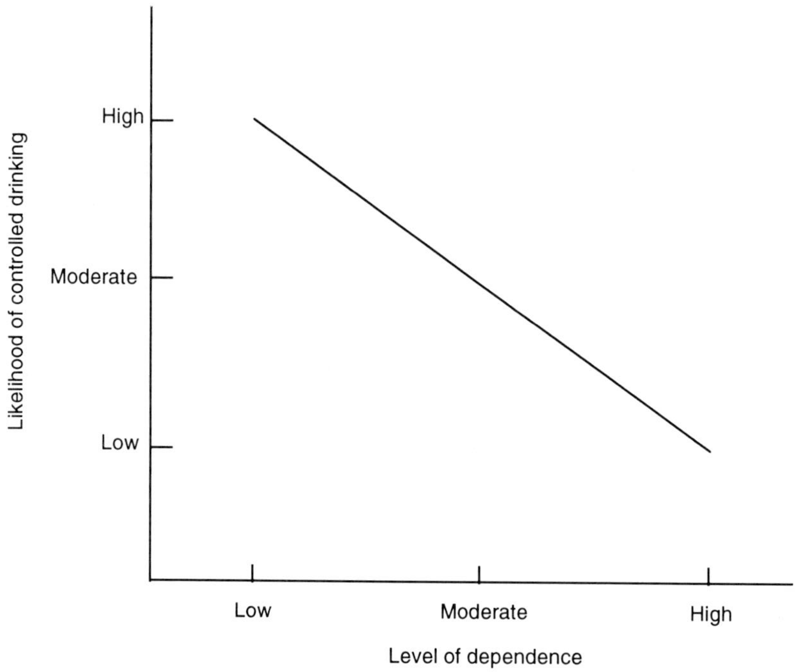

Source: Heather *(73)*. Reproduced by permission of Carfax Publishing Company, P.O. Box 25, Abingdon, Oxfordshire, United Kingdom.

We should not conclude that research will have nothing more to say on this topic. Although several studies have found rates of moderate drinking to be lower in severely dependent than in moderately or mildly dependent problem drinkers *(72),* others have found no relationship between the level of dependence and drinking outcome *(74,75)*. Moreover, most of the studies finding low rates of moderation in severely dependent individuals have addressed the effects of abstinence-oriented treatment, in which the idea of moderate drinking may have been actively discouraged, if not ridiculed. It is also possible that the development of more powerful methods of moderation training, based perhaps on theoretical and research advances, will result in more successful outcome among the more severely affected.

A Consensus on Drinking Goals

The current consensus on abstinence or moderation is based on the primary importance of the client's preferences regarding drinking goals. Certainly, if a client shows a preference for total abstinence for whatever reason, the therapist should immediately accept it. No advocate of moderation should seek to change the mind of someone who has decided that abstinence is the best policy.

On the other hand, clients may choose to aim for moderation in circumstances in which it involves considerable risks. They may already have suffered some organic damage that makes further drinking particularly hazardous, or they may show a level of alcohol dependence that makes the attainment and maintenance of moderation extremely difficult. In these cases, all the therapist can do is strongly to advise the client that abstinence would be the wisest option. If the client insists on pursuing moderation, the therapist should not turn him or her away with instructions to return only after regaining his or her senses. This happened all too often in the past. Rather, the therapist should help the client as efficiently as possible to achieve his or her chosen goal. A therapist can always revise the decision if the client relapses to excessive drinking; indeed, a bargain can be struck at the outset that, if consistent moderation has not been achieved by a certain date, the client would seriously consider switching to the abstinence option. Who can be sure that a client will necessarily fail? The client's intuitive understanding of the most suitable drinking goal may be better than the therapist's.

Unfortunately, many clients are not sure which goal they wish to pursue and look to the therapist for guidance on this key decision. The second element of the consensus on drinking goals is that this guidance should reflect the evidence that moderation is more suited to those with less serious problems, defined either by the extent and severity of alcohol-related problems or, more theoretically, by the level of alcohol dependence. Thus, the client's choice of a drinking goal should in general be matched to the level of dependence or problems. Table 3 gives criteria for this decision based on the client's measured level of dependence *(76)*. (Table 3 also refers to the decision about brief versus intensive treatment, dealt with in Chapter 7.)

Table 3. Guidelines for the goal and intensity of treatment according to level of alcohol dependence

Score			Level of dependence	Goal and intensity of treatment
Severity of alcohol-dependence questionnaire *(41)*	Alcohol dependence scale *(43)*	Short-form alcohol dependence data questionnaire *(44)*		
0–20	0–13	0–9	Low	Brief, moderate drinking intervention
21–40	14–30	10–19	Moderate	Brief or intensive intervention, moderate drinking or abstinence
41–60	31–51	20–45	High	Intensive, abstinence intervention

Source: Heather *(76)*.

As made clear earlier, the principle that clients showing a severe level of dependence should normally be advised to abstain is based less on hard and fast evidence than on the most prudent interpretation of the evidence currently available. Some evidence justifies exceptions to this principle. For example. Polich et al. *(77)* found that young, single, male problem drinkers with severe dependence were less likely to relapse if they had chosen moderation than if they had chosen abstinence; conversely, older, married, male clients with low levels of dependence were more likely to succeed with abstinence. Thus the suggestions in Table 3 should be regarded only as general guidance on drinking goals, not as inflexible rules. Besides age, gender and marital status, other variables may complicate the picture: for example, particular features of the employment situation that make either abstinence or moderate drinking less realistic, or the attitude of the client's spouse towards either goal. Above all, it should be remembered that the choice of a drinking goal is a clinical decision, depending crucially on the unique circumstances, idiosyncrasies, needs and aspirations of the individual client.

With moderate dependence, choosing the drinking goal becomes more difficult. Although the likelihood of abstinence being adopted should increase through this middle range, factors other than the level of dependence assume more significance. Again, the overriding importance of the client's preferences must be borne in mind; to impose a treatment goal on anyone who is reluctant to accept it is a waste of time. Although the client may not express definite preferences about the treatment goal, he or she may have certain beliefs about the nature of problem drinking and its treatment, and research has suggested that such beliefs have an important bearing on the prospects for successful abstinence or moderation *(74)*. Clearly, if the client believes alcoholism to be an irreversible disease based on a constitutional inability to drink normally, abstinence should be preferred. The therapist's views are another important factor; the therapist or counsellor should always believe in the validity of the treatment method being used, including the viability of the drinking goal.

Other Non-abstinent Goals

So far the goal of moderation (or "controlled drinking") has been discussed with the implication that drinking should be completely free of alcohol-related harm. This, however, may be a somewhat idealized concept; the drinking of few regular consumers of alcohol who do not seek or need treatment is unlikely to be devoid of problems, although these are usually only mild and infrequent. Moreover, certain types of client who seek help are sometimes unlikely to achieve a pattern of drinking without associated problems. All this argues for the postulation of treatment drinking goals in which some continuing presence of alcohol-related problems is tolerated.

Pattison *(78)* proposed the concept of attenuated drinking as a deliberate goal of treatment for clients who the therapist has good reasons to believe will never be able to sustain abstinence for any worthwhile length of time, and for whom the goal of harm-free drinking is unrealistic. These are mainly skid-row problem drinkers who show such major dysfunctions as part of their lifestyle that there would be little possibility of large improvements in adjustment even if they were sober. In short, these are people who probably see no benefits from giving up or radically reducing their alcohol consumption, even if they could do it. For these clients, there is a strong argument for giving precedence in treatment to modest gains in health, work and social relationships over radical changes in drinking behaviour.

The concept of attenuated drinking fits well with the more modern interest in harm reduction as applying to the prevention and treatment of problems arising from all drugs, not merely alcohol *(79)*. The harm reduction philosophy is based on the assumption that to place unrealistic expectations or demands on many clients – demands that arise from ideological and moral views of drinking rather than scientific evidence – is to do them a great disservice. For example, in the case of homeless street drinkers, the least that can and should be done is to try to keep them alive and as healthy as possible by occasional detoxification and medical attention, even though an immediate return to heavy drinking can be confidently expected.

The idea of harm reduction is applicable to all clients in assessing the effects of treatment. While the perfectionist goal of total abstinence or completely harm-free drinking may not have been achieved, valuable degrees of improvement may have occurred in many clients. Thus, the underlying goal of all treatment – significantly improving the client's life – may have been met, even if the strict drinking goals of the programme have not. It has been argued that treatment programmes can only be regarded as cost-effective if these less-than-perfect outcomes are taken into account *(80)*. Unfortunately, therapists often tend to rely on excessively strict definitions of successful treatment and relapse – to regard any drinking by a graduate of an abstinence programme as relapse and any episode of intoxication in a graduate of a moderation programme as evidence of treatment failure. Heather & Tebbutt *(81)* have argued for the use of standard definitions of categories such as abstinence, non-problem drinking and drinking but improved, and have proposed a scheme for classifying the results of treatment that allows various degrees of improvement to be recorded (Fig. 2).

Drinking Goals Among Those not Seeking Treatment

So far, this section has discussed drinking goals for problem drinkers who are attending a treatment centre for help. As part of the broadening of the base of treatment mentioned in Chapter 1, however, there is now great interest in the potential of brief interventions for excessive drinkers who do not seek help but are recruited mainly by screening in a variety of community settings.

The moderation goal has had its greatest impact here. Indeed, interest in brief interventions is unlikely to have arisen without the developments in controlled drinking treatment that occurred in the 1970s. While a preference for abstinence should always be respected, the great majority of people recruited opportunistically would immediately reject advice to abstain. They would respond only to an intervention that allowed them to continue to drink, albeit at much reduced levels. Thus, the moderation goal has fitted very well with the move towards a public health perspective on alcohol problems in society.

Chapter 7 covers the types of intervention included in this category in more detail. Here we may note that they all rely on concepts such as sensible or responsible drinking. These terms are usually defined by the limits recommended by medical authorities as representing low-risk alcohol consumption. They therefore vary from country to country and are expressed by reference to local beverages and drinking customs. The use of these sensible drinking guidelines, however, enables brief interventions to combine in their effects with health education initiatives aimed at the general public. This integrates the secondary prevention of drinking problems with primary prevention.

Benefits of the Moderation Goal

The main advantage of including the moderation goal in treatment policy is that drinkers with less serious problems can be persuaded to change their behaviour. As witnessed by the AA concept of rock

Fig. 2. Scheme to classify the outcome of treatment of alcohol problems

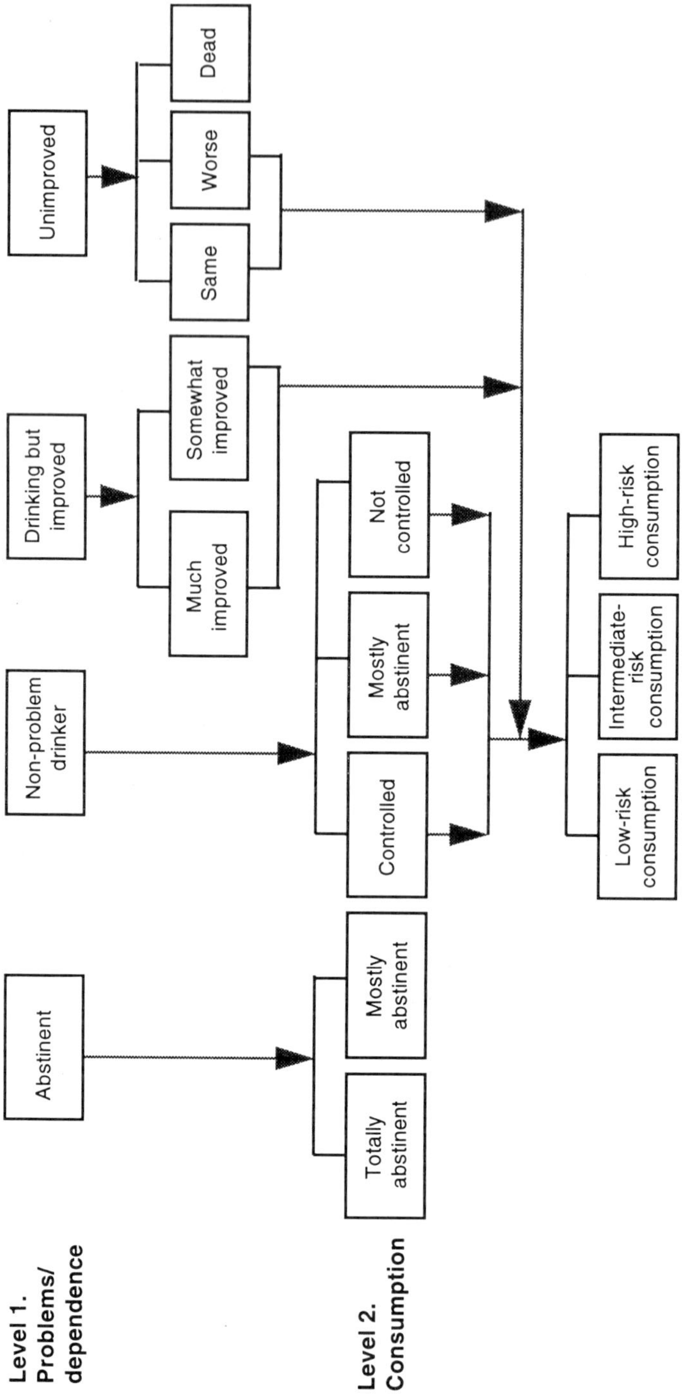

Source: Heather & Tebbutt *(81)*.

bottom, drinkers usually need to have caused a great deal of damage to themselves, their families and others, and to have experienced much pain as a result, before they are prepared to consider seriously the radical solution of forswearing alcohol for life. If people with less serious problems are led to believe that total and lifelong abstinence is the only solution to a drinking problem, they are likely to deny having a problem in the first place. (Indeed, an exclusive preoccupation in the educational literature with the most devastating consequences of chronic alcoholism supports them in this.) If people are told what the evidence clearly shows – that some problem drinkers can reduce their drinking to moderate levels – many are likely to find convincing reasons to try to do so.

Many of those with less serious problems, although by no means all, develop more serious problems over time. Thus, the moderation goal serves the interests of early intervention and secondary prevention, particularly in its application in brief, community-based intervention. This leaves those who either continue to drink at about the same heavy level or eventually reduce their drinking spontaneously, without the benefit of intervention. Estimating the size of these groups is difficult, but they comprise large numbers of drinkers *(3)*. Further, the current problems of such people are still of concern. As explained in Chapter 1, the large number of these individuals makes the alcohol problems that they show a considerable burden on society. The moderation goal thus serves the interests of reducing the total aggregate of alcohol-related harm in the population, and forms part of the public health perspective on alcohol problems.

In addition to those with less serious problems, the moderation goal benefits more seriously affected drinkers. Provided there are no contraindications, it increases the range of options available. As already suggested, many problems drinkers refuse to countenance total abstinence and others have failed several times to achieve it in treatment. In countries with progressively fewer abstainers on religious or moral grounds, total abstinence is becoming more statistically deviant in society and may be increasingly hard to sustain. The restriction on social life that abstinence imposes may well be too difficult for many clients to tolerate. For these reasons, the moderation goal has an important part to play among people seeking treatment for alcohol problems.

6

Setting of Treatment

Later chapters consider types of treatment approach and the research evidence that supports them. A discussion of where treatment should take place should come first, however, since it addresses treatment in general, irrespective of the type offered. The main issue here is the relative advantages and disadvantages of inpatient versus outpatient treatment or, to widen the context, residential versus non-residential treatment. The latter category includes outpatient and day patient treatment. Intervention can take place in other settings, too.

RESIDENTIAL VERSUS NON-RESIDENTIAL TREATMENT

Various arguments might be advanced to support the merits of either residential or non-residential treatment. One might claim, for example, that inpatient treatment provides a better opportunity for a deep analysis of the client's problems or more time to confront and wear down denial. On the other hand, one could claim that, since the problems have evolved in the client's usual environment, he or she must remain in contact with that environment while drinking behaviour is modified, and there is little point in transporting him or her to some unfamiliar residential situation elsewhere. People who favour a social learning perspective on alcohol problems would use the second argument, and many problem drinkers do not experience much desire for alcohol in hospital. They often feel confident of being cured, only to relapse very quickly as soon as they return home.

Such arguments can only be satisfactorily settled in one way: by well designed research directly comparing outcomes from residential and non-residential alternatives. Fortunately, the fairly extensive body of research on this topic provides a clear answer.

Miller & Hester *(82)* and Annis *(83)* reviewed the relevant research, and nothing has occurred subsequently to alter their conclusions *(5)*. Miller & Hester listed 12 research comparisons of residential with some form of non-residential treatment (mainly outpatient or day patient care). All these studies employed either randomization or careful group matching; most included extended follow-up, and all were conducted with problem drinkers who would otherwise have been assigned to inpatient treatment. In nearly all cases, the researchers expected to find that the residential alternative was superior.

All these studies showed the same results: residential treatment conferred no advantages over non-residential treatment. If anything, the non-residential treatment produced better results, and this superiority was recently shown to be statistically significant in a meta-analysis of the results by Mattick & Jarvis *(5)*. This putative superiority for non-residential treatment is not the main point, however; whether or not this superiority is accepted, these results show non-residential treatment to be much more cost-effective than residential treatment. The reason is simple. Inpatient treatment and other forms of residential care are much more expensive than non-residential alternatives; estimates vary but one calculation is that it is on average 10 times more expensive *(82)*. If two forms of treatment produce roughly the same results, but one is very much more costly than the other, it is obvious which one a rational treatment policy should prefer.

Exceptions to the Rule

The conclusion that non-residential treatment is to be preferred to residential treatment should be seen as a general rule, which has some exceptions. The need for inpatient, medicated detoxification in severe cases of alcohol withdrawal was already mentioned in Chapter 2. Clients who suffer from physical or psychiatric illness that requires inpatient attention comprise another straightforward exception. Yet another is homeless clients who clearly need decent hostel accommodation if they are to have much chance of improvement. In addition, special home circumstances (such as the possibility of violence) may make inpatient treatment desirable.

None of the justifications for residential treatment just listed is directly concerned with the nature of the alcohol problem or dependence itself. They all refer to matters that are independent of the treatment of alcohol problems *per se*. Nevertheless, people with a very high level of alcohol dependence and very severe alcohol-related problems may benefit more from inpatient than from outpatient treatment, perhaps because they need a complete break from the environment in which their problems have developed, so that they can put their lives back in order.

This last statement is not based on any convincing evidence but is a reasonable hypothesis about how the distinction between residential and non-residential treatment can be matched to characteristics of problem drinkers. Research is urgently needed to test this hypothesis and possibly others on matching to the setting of treatment. Research should also examine the effectiveness of different forms of non-residential treatment, such as outpatient and day patient treatment. No matter whether this research is carried out or what its results might be, non-residential treatment should be preferred for cost-effective treatment of the great majority of problem drinkers.

THE COMMUNITY

The broadening of the professional groups involved in the delivery of treatment for alcohol problems has been mentioned several times. Although alcohol specialists will continue to have an essential role, generalist workers who include (or can be persuaded to include) counselling and advice for problem drinkers with all their other duties are becoming increasingly important. Along with this expansion of personnel, there is a concomitant expansion of community settings in which treatment or counselling takes place.

The most obvious of these settings is the premises of the general practitioner (GP) and the wards and emergency departments of the general hospital (regarding these medical settings for present purposes as part of the community). As well as medical personnel, practice and community nurses have a vital role here. Another group of settings is related to the social services and involves the work of social workers of various types.

In the criminal justice area, probation officers or their equivalents in various countries are involved, and there may be special provisions for people who commit alcohol-related offences such as drink-driving. Prisons and institutions for young offenders are also an important class of setting for alcohol-related counselling, because many of the inmates are found to have alcohol-related problems that are often the main factor in their offences *(84)*. Little is likely to be achieved in the artificial environment of the prison, and a preparation for release involving arrangements for further contact outside prison is probably the best policy here. Chapter 14 addresses the difficult issue of the ethics of coerced treatment for offenders.

Finally, the workplace is a most important setting. While in most countries a high proportion of the population visits a GP each year, some people (particularly young males) do not, and the workplace represents a further opportunity for early intervention and secondary prevention. In the past, workplace interventions for alcohol problems, especially those coming under the heading of employee assistance programmes, were based on an alcoholism model and attempted to detect and treat serious alcohol-related problems encountered in the workplace. More recently, however, advice and counselling on drinking behaviour have been integrated with other health promotion activity, such as advice on smoking, physical exercise, diet and stress *(85)*. The employee with serious problems should not be neglected; merely, the opportunity should be taken to use the workplace setting to introduce a range of interventions against excessive alcohol consumption.

This not only assists primary and secondary prevention but also aims to improve productivity. The evidence clearly shows that excessive drinking makes a significant contribution towards lost productivity in the form of absenteeism, accidents and reduced work efficiency. Some evidence suggests that workplace programmes can help to redress this situation. Ethical issues are involved in workplace intervention and these are discussed in Chapter 14.

More Intensive Interventions in Community Settings

Some generalist workers may take a special interest in alcohol problems and wish to take on more serious cases (see Chapter 15). This applies principally to GPs. Research suggests that they should not be discouraged from doing so, provided they receive adequate support and advice from specialists.

Drummond et al. *(86)* consecutively assigned 40 problem drinkers, following assessment, brief advice and counselling in a clinic, to receive treatment either at a specialist clinic or from their own GPs. At follow-up after six months, both groups showed significant reductions in consumption and problems, and the results from each setting were remarkably similar. No differential effect was found for the people with higher levels of dependence.

The main drawback of this study is that the numbers were small, and it should ideally be repeated with a larger sample. Also, although there was no evidence that those showing more severe dependence benefited more from specialist treatment, the average level of dependence was relatively low and it would be accurate to describe these clients as of mainly moderate dependence (see Chapter 15). The conclusions might have been different with a more severely dependent sample with chronic problems. Finally, one should note the use of initial assessment and brief counselling in the clinic before referral back to GPs, and the provision of ongoing advice and support to GPs during treatment.

THE HOME

The indications for home detoxification were discussed in Chapter 2, and intervention such as counselling by social workers or community nurses could take place in the client's home. This setting also provides an opportunity for a different kind of intervention: the use of self-help manuals by problem drinkers.

There is good evidence that self-help manuals can be effective, either as an adjunct or an alternative to counselling, or as a form of continued intervention after counselling. When they are an alternative to counselling, clients can be recruited by advertisements in newspapers and other media *(87)*. Clearly, the targets for self-help manuals distributed in this way are drinkers with hazardous consumption and those with relatively low levels of alcohol dependence. For this reason, manuals should state clearly at the outset that they are not intended for people with serious problems, and should also include in an appendix a list of addresses of treatment agencies. Nevertheless, problem drinkers who live in remote areas with no accessible treatment services may derive benefit from self-help manuals. They may also be useful to problem drinkers who are unwilling to attend treatment agencies because of a special sensitivity to the stigma of admitting an alcohol problem *(88)*.

Most self-help manuals published so far have been based on cognitive–behavioural principles and are essentially condensations of behavioural self-control training (see Chapter 10). This need not necessarily be the case, and other types of self-help manual may be preferred in particular countries. Probably the most important principle is that the self-help manual should reflect the drinking customs and other cultural nuances of drinking in the population for whom it is intended.

7

Length and Intensity of Treatment: Brief Interventions

An implicit assumption in the alcohol field is that the more treatment, the better; that is, the longer or more intensively the client receives treatment, the greater his or her chances of recovery. This assumption was challenged in the previous chapter, which showed that inpatient or other residential treatment, involving more intensive contact with the client, was not superior to outpatient or other forms of non-residential treatment. This chapter continues the challenge with evidence that treatment of longer duration or higher intensity is often no more effective than that of shorter duration or lesser intensity. (Intensity refers to variations in the amount of treatment contact within a given period of time.)

DURATION OF TREATMENT AND OUTCOME

One reason for the supposition that more treatment is better than less, is the observation that clients who stay longer in a programme tend to do better than those who discharge themselves or are discharged for other reasons earlier on. Indeed, uncontrolled research supports the idea of a positive relationship between length of stay and outcome *(3)*. The problems of interpretation here are obvious: those who stay longer in treatment are likely to be better motivated to succeed, to be more compliant with the treatment regime, or to possess other characteristics associated with favourable prognosis. The results of controlled research, in which clients are randomly assigned to receive longer or shorter forms of treatment, give a very different picture.

Miller & Hester *(1,82)* list four controlled evaluations of long and short inpatient treatment. None of these showed any superiority for longer treatment at follow-up and, as with residential versus non-residential treatment, the shorter programmes showed, if anything, better results. (Long and short in this context mean more and less than four weeks inpatient stay, respectively.) The preceding chapter showed that inpatient stays should no longer be regarded as the staple form of treatment for alcohol problems, and this research is therefore of little practical interest. Nevertheless, it clearly reinforces the more general point that more treatment is not the same as better treatment.

The evidence bearing on the duration of outpatient treatment is not quite as clear as that for the inpatient variety. Miller & Hester *(1)* argue that, when attention is confined to only those studies that use the preferred methodological option of random assignment to groups (rather than group matching), no support for the superior effectiveness of extended outpatient treatment can be discerned. Here we are beginning to encroach on a special topic of much current interest and practical significance: the effectiveness and cost–effectiveness of so-called brief interventions for alcohol problems. The remainder of this chapter addresses this important topic.

BRIEF INTERVENTIONS

The term brief interventions refers to a family of interventions that are difficult to define exclusively but share some central features: they are of shorter duration or lower intensity and are cheaper to implement than conventional treatment interventions *(76)*. If conducted by an alcohol specialist, brief interventions consist of fewer or less frequent sessions – probably far fewer – than normal treatment. They are often conducted by generalist workers, however, in the kinds of non-specialist setting discussed in the previous chapter: general medical practice, hospital wards, social work settings, criminal justice settings, and the workplace. To encourage busy professionals to implement these interventions and integrate them with a multitude of other duties, they must be brief and user-friendly.

The target population for brief interventions ranges from people showing only potential alcohol-related problems (hazardous drinkers) to those with moderately serious problems. Similarly, it covers the range from mild to moderately severe alcohol dependence. A conservative and prudent recommendation is that people with serious problems or severe dependence should normally be directed to conventional, specialized treatment. Fig. 3 shows a suggested relationship between the type of intervention and the seriousness of alcohol-related problems. This reinforces the point of an increasingly specialized treatment response for a decreasing number of people with progressively more serious problems. A major omission from Fig. 3, however, is the notion that brief interventions may also be suitable for hazardous drinkers (defined purely in terms of consumption level) with no obvious alcohol-related problems.

Fig. 3. Relationship between the severity of alcohol problems and the type of intervention needed

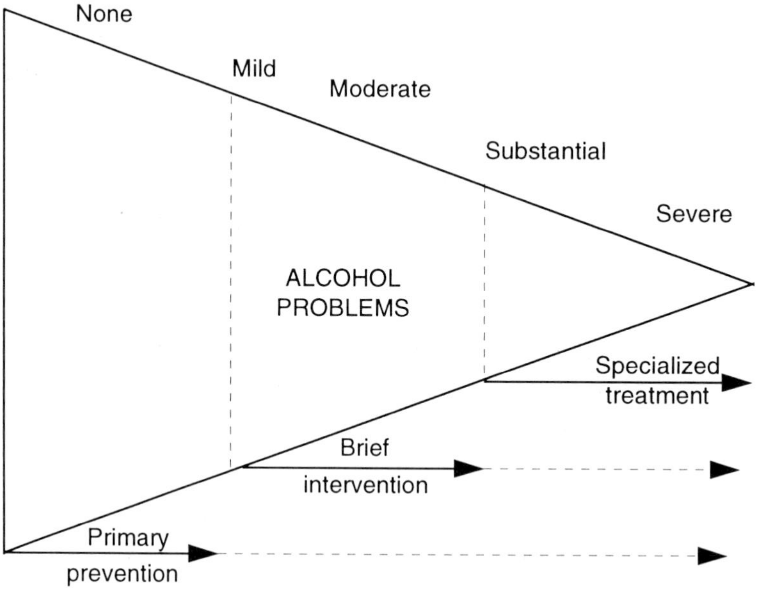

Source: Institute of Medicine *(3)*. Reproduced by permission of National Academy Press, Washington, DC, USA.

The guidelines implied in Fig. 3 are only general rules, to which exceptions exist. Some people with only moderate problems may need a more intensive approach, and some with serious problems may benefit from brief intervention.

REASONS FOR INTEREST IN BRIEF INTERVENTIONS

A summary of the historical and other background factors that have stimulated interest in brief interventions may indicate their significance. One of the key events in this history was the publication in 1977 of the results of a treatment trial conducted by Orford & Edwards *(89)* at the Maudsley Hospital, London. These authors randomly assigned 100 married, male problem drinkers to receive conventional inpatient or outpatient treatment, complete with the full panoply of services available at a leading psychiatric institution, or to a single three-hour assessment and advice session for each client and his wife. At follow-up one and two years later, these groups showed no statistically significant differences. This finding was repeated in subsequent follow-ups of this cohort up to 12 years after treatment *(90)*.

The results of this study had a profound effect on the treatment of alcohol problems, leading to a greater pessimism about the efficacy of treatment proper and even a debate as to whether treatment could be said to work at all. While such a nihilistic interpretation of Orford & Edwards' research has in general been abandoned, many subsequent studies have supported its main implication that brief, inexpensive intervention can often be as effective as a conventional, full treatment programme.

Another important influence at about the same time was the study by Russell et al. *(91)* of the effects of GPs' advice against cigarette smoking. Conducted in the London area, the study found that a group of people advised to stop smoking, given a leaflet to help them try and warned that they would be followed up had a superior quit rate one year later than either a group given only simple advice or two control groups. While this quit rate (continuous abstinence) was only 5.1% the authors calculated that, if the successful intervention were applied by all GPs in the United Kingdom, this would result in over 500 000 ex-smokers per year, a figure that could not be equalled by increasing the number of specialist withdrawal clinics to 10 000. Many further studies of GPs' advice against smoking have confirmed the original promise of the study by Russell et al. and have refined and improved the brief intervention technique. The alcohol field has borrowed the logic and methodology of this line of research.

Other influences have conspired to focus attention on brief interventions. The advent of the goals of controlled drinking as a respectable part of treatment policy, in some quarters at least, enabled intervention to become much more acceptable to people with less severe problems. At the same time, the move from an alcoholism model to the new public health perspective on alcohol problems in society created a ready-made role for brief interventions. Finally, all this coincided with increasingly fierce competition by various sectors of health care for limited resources, with the resultant insistence by the holders of the purse-strings that interventions be shown to be as cost-effective as possible (see Chapter 13).

Evidence for Effectiveness

In considering the evidence for the effectiveness of brief interventions, one should make a most important distinction at the outset: the distinction between their use with people who are actively seeking help for a problem with alcohol and those who are not seeking help but have been opportunistically identified as drinking excessively by some sort of screening procedure in a non-specialist setting *(76).*

Population not Seeking Treatment

The evidence for the effectiveness of brief interventions is far stronger among the population not seeking treatment than among problem drinkers presenting at treatment agencies. Based on the model of Russell et al. *(91),* the logic of research in this area is straightforward: the comparison of the effects on drinking behaviour, preferably in a randomized controlled trial, of a brief intervention with a non-intervention control group and/or of an even more minimal intervention. A collection of studies conducted in different parts of the world has shared this type of design *(92–94)* and has found evidence in favour of the brief intervention, at least among men. Among women, those in both intervention and control groups showed marked reductions in consumption, possibly because women are more sensitive to the effects of assessment *(94,95).* A recent meta-analysis of the studies that could be grouped together as reporting changes in alcohol consumption *(96)* estimated the treatment effect of brief intervention among both sexes to be about 7 United Kingdom units of alcohol per week (1 unit equals about 9 g ethanol), or a 23% reduction in alcohol consumption.

The most impressive recent results come from a randomized clinical trial, coordinated by WHO, of brief interventions in primary health care in 10 countries: Australia, Bulgaria, Costa Rica, Kenya, Mexico, Norway, the United Kingdom, the United States, the former USSR and Zimbabwe *(94)*. The results showed that, among men, an assessment of 20 minutes plus 5 minutes' simple advice was more effective in leading to reduced consumption than the assessment alone. Adding a further 15 minutes of counselling to the simple advice, or even offering extended counselling over three further sessions, did not improve results.

Although the WHO study has provided firm evidence of the effectiveness of brief interventions among men, it would be perilous to conclude that all recipients of brief interventions need only 5 minutes' simple advice. The next chapter provides the justification for this statement.

Population Seeking Treatment

Evidence to support the widespread application of brief interventions to the population seeking treatment is far less convincing, although these interventions probably have an important part to play. In the first place, studies in this area are based on a comparison of a brief intervention with a more intensive treatment alternative, so the evidence adduced in support of the brief intervention is a failure to find a significant superiority of the conventional treatment. Owing to the logic of statistical hypothesis testing, however, it is very difficult to prove that two forms of treatment have the same effect; all that can be concluded from a single study is that these particular results give no evidence that the brief and intensive interventions differ in effect. Unfortunately, many of the studies in this area have had very small sample sizes, and this may have prevented the emergence of an effect of conventional treatment. Research in this area has several other methodological problems that limit the conclusions that can be drawn *(5,97)*.

Conclusions on Usefulness

Nevertheless, the evidence that some clients can benefit from brief or less intensive treatment, and do not appear to need conventional treatment, is sufficient to justify a place for brief interventions in a modern treatment service. In this situation, it is advisable to err, if anywhere, on the side of caution.

A prudent policy for people seeking treatment is largely to reserve brief interventions for those with less serious problems and/or mild degrees of dependence. Table 3 suggests the two extremes of the continuum of dependence at which either intensive or brief treatment should normally be preferred. Like the selection of a drinking goal, however, this is a clinical decision and there may well be exceptions to the general rule. For some individual reason some people with relatively less serious problems may need a more intensive intervention, and some with more serious problems may need a brief intervention, perhaps because they choose it. An alternative and conservative policy is the stepped care approach described in Chapter 15. In addition, subsequent research, improvements in behaviour change technology, and clinical experience with brief interventions may lead to revisions of the position adopted here.

There is nothing unethical or uncaring about offering brief interventions to suitable clients. This is sometimes difficult for treatment providers to accept if they are firmly wedded to practising intensive treatment. Nevertheless, the facts simply contradict this understandable commitment to intensive treatment for all clients. It could even be argued that failure to offer brief interventions is unethical, since it represents a waste of precious resources that could more profitably be directed towards providing a greater number of clients with less intensive intervention and ensuring proper assistance to those who need more attention. An efficient follow-up monitoring system, which can serve as a safety net to catch those who have not benefited from a brief intervention and can be offered a more intensive alternative, can considerably decrease any possible ethical misgivings about providing brief interventions (see Chapter 15).

The difference between the treatment-seeking and other populations in the recommended use of brief interventions should not cause surprise. People seeking treatment typically have far more serious problems and higher levels of dependence than those identified by screening. At the same time, the treatment seekers, even those who have been pressured by spouses or others to attend treatment, are likely to be better motivated to abstain or cut down than those who probably have to be persuaded that a problem exists. This higher average level of motivation may make many clients more responsive to conventional treatment or liable to be disappointed with a brief contact. In addition, unknown and unmeasured differences between populations that are defined in very different ways may affect treatment response.

Types of Brief Intervention

Although it is useful for some purposes to think of brief interventions as a single category, they vary greatly in length, structure, particular targets, media of communication and personnel responsible for delivery. They also differ in the underpinning philosophy and the theory of behavioural change, implicit or explicit, on which they are based. Brief interventions are therefore best regarded as a family of interventions rather than a single entity. As with conventional treatment, the important task is to select the right kind of intervention for each kind of client and delivery situation.

This section examines some types of brief intervention that have been developed and tested. In view of the large number and diversity of these interventions, however, only a short and selective summary can be given; the interested reader should consult the original texts. Heather *(76)* offers a general review of this area.

The first intervention to be described was the basic treatment scheme, arising from the comparison of treatment and advice by Orford & Edwards *(89)*. This consists of four elements:

- a comprehensive assessment;
- a single, detailed counselling session for the client and, when the client is in a close relationship, the partner;
- some follow-up system to check on progress; and
- common reasons for going beyond the basic approach.

The first two parts take about three hours. This basic scheme was developed in conjunction with abstinence-oriented treatment, but it could be adapted to treatment with moderation as a goal. Although originally described nearly 20 years ago, it is still highly relevant to modern practice.

Despite its merits, the basic treatment scheme is based on clinical experience and common sense; it does not depend on any particular theoretical approach to behavioural change. A more theoretical form of brief intervention that can be used by treatment agencies represents a kind of condensed form of cognitive–behavioural therapy (see Chapter 10). Sanchez-Craig et al. *(98)* have described the theory behind this kind of approach and its associated methods and outlined a minimal form of this type of intervention. Zweben et al. *(99)* developed a brief form of behavioural marital therapy that was no less successful than a conventional version of this form of treatment. In addition, many self-help manuals *(100,101)* in the field are based on cognitive–behavioural principles, and agency-based therapists can use them as both guides to brief intervention and supplements for the client to use at home.

Brief interventions used in community settings, such as general medical practice or other primary care settings, have usually been briefer or less intensive than those provided by treatment agencies. This is another reason for making a clear distinction between the two classes of brief intervention. In some cases, the term minimal intervention is probably more appropriate. For example, the intervention found effective in the WHO project mentioned above *(94)* took only 5 minutes of a health adviser's time, although it was preceded by 20 minutes of assessment, which may also have had some therapeutic effect. This kind of intervention aims to communicate clear advice about problem drinking, based on an individual assessment *(94)*. Perhaps the most important aspect of this advice is the provision of sensible drinking limits for people who choose not to abstain. These depend on the specific recommendations of medical authorities in each country but are usually around 3–4 standard drinks per occasion for men and 2–3 standard drinks per occasion for women (1 standard drink equals about 10 g ethanol), with the additional rule of 2–3 days of abstinence per week.

Busy physicians or other primary health care workers, who would not have time for a more prolonged intervention, could apply this minimal intervention. Despite the results of the WHO project, there are grounds for believing that a somewhat more extensive type of intervention by those who have the time and inclination to do so could produce additional benefits. Several research projects have found some evidence for the effectiveness of interventions consisting of about four or five consultations with a primary health care physician or nurse *(92,93,102)*. This type of approach relies heavily on the self-monitoring of alcohol consumption, the identification of high-risk situations for excessive drinking (see Chapter 10), the formulation of simple rules to establish control over drinking, and the discussion of alternatives to drinking as part of a healthier lifestyle. Feedback of gamma-glutamyltransferase (GGT), as pioneered by Kristenson et al. *(103)* in Sweden, is also an important element of this more prolonged approach. Other ingredients converge with the motivational approach to intervention, which is discussed in the next chapter. The evidence suggests that clients gain most of the benefit from brief interventions involving repeat visits during the first two or three sessions, and that additional sessions are redundant.

Compared with the general practice setting, the hospital ward offers more time for screening and intervention among the excessive drinkers who may be encountered there: up to 40% of inpatients, depending on the type of ward in question *(104)*. Chick et al. *(105)* describe a single session of counselling given by an experienced nurse and lasting up to one hour. The main objective is for the client to weigh up the advantages and disadvantages of his or her current pattern of drinking and come to a decision about the future level of consumption. This has a lot in common with the motivational approach to problem drinking described in the next chapter. The interventions covered in this section can be adapted for use in other medical settings, such as accident and emergency departments. They can also be modified, by various ad hoc adjustments, for use in all the other settings that have been mentioned in this book.

Disseminating Brief Interventions

More research on opportunistic brief interventions in community settings is clearly needed before definite conclusions can be reached on several important issues. Nevertheless, the evidence for their general effectiveness is sufficient to justify their widespread use. This raises a different set of problems.

For example, many GPs are reluctant to deal with drinking problems in their practices. They may feel that this work is not a legitimate part of medical practice or that they lack the training and skills needed. Very often, when GPs think about drinking problems they conjure up the stereotype of the alcoholic, who is thought to have a hopeless prognosis and who may cause trouble in the surgery. The idea of early interventions for patients with less serious alcohol problems and a good prognosis has yet to be adequately communicated to GPs in most countries. GPs are, of course, very busy people who are constantly urged by a whole range of interested parties to take a special interest in one kind of disorder or another. Nevertheless, their active and willing cooperation is crucial to the entire strategy for using brief interventions to achieve a widespread reduction in excessive drinking in the population at large.

The question of how best to achieve the desired dissemination of brief interventions among GPs is an important research topic, and this problem has received welcome attention in recent years. For example, the WHO Regional Office for Europe has developed a project as part of the European Alcohol Action Plan: a multicentre controlled trial involving 10 countries. It will compare three methods of increasing the uptake of brief interventions by GPs (mail only, telemarketing and personal marketing), and then two levels of support for their effects on utilization of the interventions during the implementation phase. This project should provide valuable information on how to market brief interventions to GPs and how to ensure that physicians incorporate them into routine practice.

Similar considerations apply, of course, to other medical settings and all the other settings that are relevant to the application of brief interventions. We urgently need to know how best to persuade hospital physicians, occupational physicians, nurses, health visitors, social workers, probation officers and other professionals to make the provision of brief interventions a routine part of their work.

8

Increasing Motivation for Change

One of the most popular ideas in the field of alcohol problems at present is an attempt to describe how people change addictive behaviour. This is the so-called stages of change model, first described in the early 1980s by Prochaska, DiClemente and their colleagues and increasingly influential ever since.

STAGES OF CHANGE

The model was first developed as a general theory of behavioural change as part of the transtheoretical approach to psychotherapy *(46,47)*. Its main research application was in the area of smoking cessation, with particular relevance to quitting without formal help. The model's particular usefulness in understanding change in the addictions soon became clear.

The stages of change model is based on observations that people pass through similar stages and use similar processes of change when they change their behaviour in significant ways. The key concept is readiness for change, which is seen as an internal state influenced by outside factors. The traditional concept of treatment motivation can be seen as the person's readiness to change the specific behaviour in question. Another important point is that motivation and change are not linear but cyclical.

The stages of change model can be depicted in various ways, but Fig. 4 gives a version with six stages, one of which lies outside the cycle of change. The starting point is this precontemplation stage, in which a person (for example, an excessive drinker) is either unaware of a problem or sees no need for change. Perhaps because of increasing negative consequences of alcohol use, the person then moves to the contemplation stage, in which he or she weighs the advantages and disadvantages of continuing drinking at the present level against those of changing the behaviour: either cutting down or quitting drinking. In the contemplation stage, the drinker can be seen as being in a state of conflict and ambivalence about excessive drinking and the need for change. The recognition that this stage describes the motivational state of very many excessive drinkers, both those who present for treatment and those who do not, has perhaps been the most influential contribution of the stages of change model.

Fig. 4. The stages of change

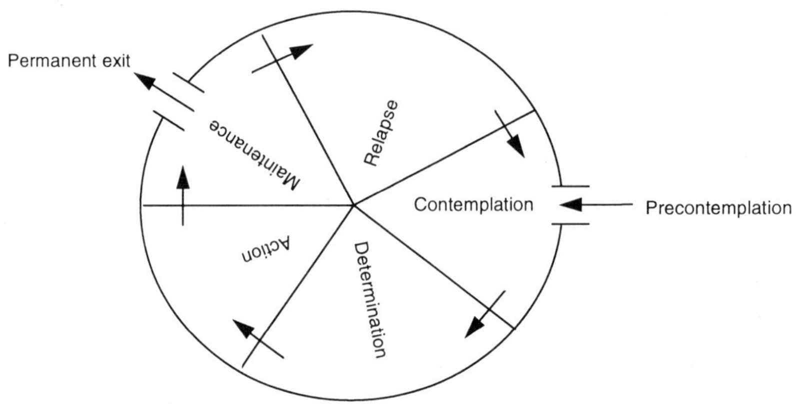

Source: Miller & Rollnick *(12)*.

Sometimes people become trapped in the conflict of the contemplation stage or even move back to precontemplation. If conditions are right, however, the drinker moves forward to the determination stage. Here, he or she makes a definite commitment to change and evaluates plans for making the change. (Determination here is very similar to a preparation stage recently described by DiClemente et al. *(106)*.) Again, if the right conditions prevail, the drinker continues to move on to the action stage, in which he or she takes specific forms of action to resolve the problem. Effecting a change in behaviour, however, does not guarantee that the change will be maintained over time. In the case of alcohol dependence and other addictions, relapse is common (see Chapter 11). In the maintenance stage, therefore, the task is to preserve the gains that have been made, which may well require a fresh set of skills and cognitive strategies. If this stage is successfully negotiated, the drinker exits the cycle of change with a permanent or at least long-lasting change in drinking behaviour. If not, the person relapses and quickly re-enters the contemplation stage, and the cycle of change resumes.

The drinker may have to take many journeys around the cycle of change before accomplishing a long-lasting resolution of a drinking problem, a fact that can be confirmed by anyone with experience of treating alcohol problems. In research by Prochaska & DiClemente *(107),* the average number of cycles completed by smokers before quitting permanently was four, and this number is likely to be of similar magnitude for excessive drinkers. Each attempt, however, seems to increase the probability of long-lasting change; in a recent publication, Prochaska et al. *(108)* refer to a spiral of change in which each completion of the cycle makes eventual success more likely.

Practical Implications of the Model

The important practical consequence of the model is that therapists or counsellors should vary their modes of intervention according to the client's current place in the cycle of change *(109).* Table 4 summarizes the main implications of each stage for the therapist. The general hypothesis here is that matching clients to appropriate forms of intervention according to their stage of change will increase overall success rates; there is some evidence to support this hypothesis in the alcohol field, but much more is needed. The corollary is that giving an intervention mismatched with the stage of change will lead to treatment failure. For example, for someone in the action stage, continued emphasis on the need for abstinence and a failure to provide practical guidance on how change can be accomplished may result in demoralization and a lost opportunity. On the other hand, plunging into specific intervention methods with someone in contemplation, who is not yet ready to change, may be perceived as irrelevant by the client and be counterproductive. This applies even more forcefully in the case of someone in precontemplation. This type of mismatch between therapist behaviour and client expectations could account for much of what is traditionally called denial and resistance in treatment. This is discussed in more detail below.

Table 4. Implication of the client's stage of change for the therapist's mode of intervention

Client stage	Therapist's motivational tasks
Precontemplation	Raising doubt – increasing the client's perception of risks and problems with current behaviour
Contemplation	Tipping the balance – evoking reasons to change and risks of not changing, and strengthening the client's self-efficacy for change of current behaviour
Determination	Helping the client to determine the best course of action to take in seeking change
Action	Helping the client to take steps towards change
Maintenance	Helping the client to identify and use strategies to prevent relapse
Relapse	Helping the client to renew the processes of contemplation, determination and action, without becoming stuck or demoralized because of relapse

Source: Miller & Rollnick *(12)*.

Assessing Stage of Change

Using these principles of treatment matching obviously requires an ability to tell where in the cycle a particular client is currently located. A skilled clinician can do this simply on the basis of clients' accounts of their problems and their responses to questions, including non-verbal responses. For many purposes, however, it is probably better to use standardized and validated measuring instruments (see also Chapter 3). Several exist; the University of Rhode Island Change Assessment (URICA) *(46)* can be applied to any behavioural problem. A short instrument specifically designed for use with opportunistic brief interventions among excessive drinkers who are not seeking treatment is the readiness to change questionnaire *(48)*; a new version of this questionnaire, intended for use with those seeking help, is under development.

MOTIVATIONAL INTERVIEWING

As suggested above, many people who present to agencies for the treatment of alcohol problems have not yet formed a definite commitment to change. Even less commitment is found, for obvious reasons, in the excessive drinkers who are identified by screening methods and who have not requested help. Even when a problem drinker appears to be convinced that some change is necessary, he or she nearly always has a lingering attachment to heavy drinking and intoxication, and a profound ambivalence towards alcohol, since conflict is an essential part of what we mean by addiction *(110)*.

These observations form the background for a relatively new approach to treating alcohol problems or, rather, a style of interaction with problem drinkers that can be used in conjunction with any approach to treatment. This is motivational interviewing *(12)*, which has been developed over the last decade by William R. Miller and his co-workers and has become increasingly widely used. It is one of the most important, if not the most important, innovation in the field in recent times.

Before exploring what motivational interviewing is, describing what it definitely is not is useful. This permits a clear contrast to be made with a traditional style of interaction that is still influential.

The Confrontational Approach

A traditional view in the field is that an alcoholic is someone who shows denial of his or her disease of alcoholism, resistance to being helped to overcome it and a number of other defence mechanisms, all aimed at insulating the person from reality and the need for change. These defence mechanisms are said to be deeply ingrained in the alcoholic's character structure and, indeed, definitive of the condition of alcoholism. As a result, the alcoholic client is regarded as a habitual liar who cannot be trusted to cooperate with treatment. Moreover, his or her lack of contact with reality can be used as a justification for treatment against his or her will (see Chapter 14). The only possible way of overcoming the alcoholic's rigid defences is to batter him or her into submission and an acceptance of the label of alcoholism by a process of aggressive confrontation with the reality of the situation.

Given the popularity of this approach, the lack of any evidence whatever to support it is surprising. Problem drinkers at all levels of severity do not appear to show more denial or resistance than people without drinking problems, and those who accept the label of alcoholism appear to do no better, and may actually do worse, than those who reject it *(12)*. When compared with alternative approaches to counselling, confrontation has been found to be less effective and to be harmful for clients with low self-esteem *(64)*. Although often associated with the twelve-step philosophy, the confrontational approach as usually practised runs entirely counter to the spirit of the writings of Bill Wilson, the cofounder of AA *(111)*.

In view of the lack of justifying evidence, the popularity of the confrontational approach is somewhat mysterious, but can be explained in various ways. One strong possibility is that confrontation actually engenders the very behaviour it seeks to counter, in the manner of a self-fulfilling prophecy. If the counsellor or therapist adopts a hostile and authoritarian posture towards the client, insisting that the client is fundamentally misguided and must accept everything that he or she says in order to begin the recovery process, the client is very likely to respond by denying that the problem is as serious as the counsellor or therapist makes out. In a basic psychological mechanism called reactance, people react to a perceived threat to their autonomy by a spirited assertion of their personal freedom and individuality. This response is especially likely, given the profoundly ambivalent feelings that the client usually has about alcohol use.

Hence the so-called denial and resistance shown by the client, and taken by the therapist as confirmation of a pre-existing personality disorder, is not some inherent ingredient of the client's character structure but a product of a particular kind of interaction between therapist and client. In general, motivation is not an immutable personality trait residing inside the individual that different clients possess to a greater or lesser degree. It is, to a significant extent, a variable property of the interaction between the client and the people attempting to alter his or her behaviour.

In an important piece of research, Miller et al. *(112)* have provided strong support for this interactional view of client motivation. They randomly assigned problem drinkers to receive confrontational or client-centred, motivational counselling. Clients in the confrontation group showed a much higher level of resistance during counselling sessions than those in the other group. In addition, the more confrontational the counsellor, the more the client was drinking at follow-up over a year later. This and other evidence *(12)* strongly suggest that confrontation is counterproductive in the attempt to motivate the client for treatment, and that a different approach should be preferred.

Principles and Strategies of Motivational Interviewing

It is not possible here to give anything like an adequate account of the thinking behind motivational interviewing or the guiding principles, strategies and methods that form part of this general approach to counselling in the addictions. Only the main features of motivational interviewing and its differences from other perspectives on counselling are briefly mentioned. For a detailed introduction to motivational interviewing, the interested reader should consult Miller & Rollnick *(12)*.

Motivational interviewing is a highly practical approach to counselling that aims to help clients build commitment and reach a firm decision to change harmful drinking patterns (and other addictive behaviour). It is a general method for helping people to recognize the nature of their actual or potential problems in relation to alcohol, and to take action to solve these problems. One of the keys to understanding the approach is the rule that responsibility for change lies with the client, because that is the only way in which genuine change can occur. The counsellor's overriding task is to create an atmosphere in which the client can freely explore concerns and take the first steps towards changing his or her lifestyle.

Although deriving originally from the client-centred perspective on counselling *(113)*, motivational interviewing differs from the classical, non-directive counselling style. The counsellor has a clear agenda in motivational interviewing: to direct the client subtly, persuasively and actively towards change. Although the empathic reflection of the client's concerns is a cornerstone of both client-centred counselling and motivational interviewing, the latter uses reflection selectively and combines it with a number of other techniques and skills aimed at tipping the motivational balance in the direction of change. At appropriate points, the counsellor can provide feedback on the consequences of the client's drinking, and advice when requested. Rather than passively following the client's own directions, the counsellor actively attempts to create a discrepancy between what the client is and what he or she would like to be, and strengthens the client's confidence in being able to do something about his or her drinking.

Motivational interviewing differs sharply, not only from the confrontational style of counselling, but also from the cognitive–behavioural (or skills training) approach in that it avoids teaching and prescribing specific coping strategies. Motivational interviewing can often be used as a forerunner to skills training for those clients who reach the action or maintenance stages of change. Often, however, and particularly for people whose problems are less severe, a relatively short course of motivational interviewing is all that is needed to propel the client along the path towards change. Motivational interviewing is ideally suited to clients who express ambivalence about the need to change drinking behaviour: that is, those in the contemplation stage.

Applications

Motivational interviewing is important as a general approach to counselling and to an overall style of interaction that can and should permeate all interviews with problem drinkers. Its main principles, however, have also been translated into special brief intervention programmes for specific purposes.

The first of these applications is the drinker's check-up described by Miller et al. *(114)*. They promoted the drinker's check-up through advertisements in the local news media as a health check-up focused on drinking. They stressed that:

1. the check-up would be free and completely confidential;
2. it was not part of a treatment programme;
3. it was intended for drinkers in general, not for alcoholics;

4. participants would not be labelled or diagnosed; and
5. clear and objective feedback would be given that drinkers could use as they pleased.

Thus, the intervention was made as non-threatening as possible to attract people in early stages of problems. The complete check-up required two visits, a two-hour comprehensive assessment and a return visit a week later, when clients received feedback on the assessment results as part of a motivational interview. The assessment measures included a comprehensive profile of drinking behaviour *(37)*, blood tests for the measurement of GGT and other biochemical indicators of excessive consumption, neuropsychological tests sensitive to alcohol's effects on the brain, and questions on reasons for drinking and alcohol-related problems. Thus, this intervention emphasized the feedback aspects of motivational interviewing. The results of an evaluation of the check-up were encouraging *(114)*.

Some of the ingredients of the drinker's check-up were expanded to form a brief intervention for use in Project MATCH (see page 40) and named motivational enhancement therapy *(115)*. It consists of four individualized treatment sessions spread over twelve weeks and, whenever possible, includes the client's spouse or another significant person in the client's life. The first session (in week 1) provides structured feedback from an initial assessment of problems related to drinking, level of consumption and other relevant issues, and begins the attempt to build the client's motivation. The second session (in week 2) continues the motivational enhancement process and works towards forming a definite commitment to change. The remaining two sessions (in weeks 6 and 12) are follow-up sessions, in which the therapist continues to monitor and encourage change. Outcomes from motivational enhancement therapy as used in Project MATCH should say a great deal about the effectiveness of motivational interviewing and brief interventions.

Rollnick et al. *(116)* developed another form of brief motivational interviewing for excessive drinkers identified on general hospital wards. This provides a menu of motivational strategies that generalist workers can use in a single session of counselling at the bedside, to elicit the client's concerns regarding drinking behaviour and to provide constructive feedback. As yet unpublished research has shown that brief motivational interviewing is more effective than either a skills-based approach or no intervention in assisting excessive drinkers in the contemplation stage of change to cut down their drinking after discharge from hospital.

Evidence for Motivational Interviewing

Motivational interviewing has captured the imagination of many people working in the field of alcohol problems, mainly because it makes excellent clinical sense and fits with their experience of dealing with problem drinkers. In addition, research evidence for its effectiveness is beginning to accumulate. Some of this was mentioned in the preceding section. In addition, Brown & Miller *(117)* randomly assigned 28 consecutive admissions to a private psychiatric hospital to receive or not receive a two-session motivational assessment and interview shortly after intake, in addition to the standard evaluation and treatment. The people receiving the motivational intervention participated more fully in treatment and showed a significantly lower level of alcohol consumption at follow-up after three months.

THERAPIST CHARACTERISTICS

The next five chapters examine various theoretical approaches to the treatment of alcohol problems, and compare their practical effectiveness in general and for specific types of client. Another set of factors, however, may be of equal or greater importance than the treatment approach adopted, and they apply no matter what approach is offered to the problem drinker. These concern the characteristics, not of the clients or the treatment itself, but of the therapists or counsellors giving the treatment. This topic is included in the present chapter because there is good reason to believe that these therapist characteristics affect the client's motivation for recovery.

The literature on psychotherapy and behaviour therapy has a long tradition of stressing the crucial role of non-specific factors in the treatment process. These non-specific or so-called placebo factors are said to apply to all forms of treatment and to be the common ingredients of all successful therapeutic outcomes. Of the range of non-specific factors that have been discussed in the literature, probably the most important are the therapist's characteristics and style of interaction with the client.

More specifically, Carl Rogers and his followers *(118,119)* have identified three therapist variables that they believe are largely responsible for determining whether clients improve: empathy, non-possessive warmth and genuineness. Of these, empathy has received the most attention; in this context, it means the ability accurately to reflect the client's own experience in a way that leads to further self-discovery. As mentioned, empathy is a crucial ingredient of motivational interviewing.

Evidence from the field of alcohol problems and from other areas strongly suggests that no effective treatment service can afford to ignore the importance of therapist characteristics. The evidence indicates that they account for as much, if not more, of the variance in treatment outcome as the particular type of treatment used *(12)*.

This has two major implications. First, great care should be taken to select therapists or counsellors who possess the required characteristics. Impressive formal qualifications or high academic ability are not essential; indeed, these qualities can sometimes be barriers to an effective counselling style. More important are personal attributes that have been shown to improve the quality of the therapeutic relationship. Second, these attributes are not only natural qualities of the therapist's personality but also skills that can be taught. In particular, empathy can be considerably improved by practice. This emphasizes the vital importance of effective training for counsellors in therapeutic skills.

9

Pharmacological Approaches

Perhaps the most obvious way to treat alcohol problems is to use pharmacological agents to alter behaviour, in the same way as they are used in general psychiatry to treat other behavioural and psychological disorders. This chapter considers three classes of drug that have been employed in the treatment of alcohol problems: those that sensitize the body to alcohol, those that alter the effects of alcohol and those that alter the client's mood. The use of drugs in detoxification was covered in Chapter 2.

ALCOHOL-SENSITIZING AGENTS

Drugs in this class are also known as antidipsotropic medications or, more plainly, deterrent drugs. Their purpose is to deter the problem drinker from drinking by producing a very unpleasant physiological reaction if he or she consumes alcohol. Three drugs have been used clinically for this purpose: disulfiram, calcium carbimide citrate and metronidazole. Disulfiram has had by far the most clinical use and research attention.

Disulfiram

The interaction between disulfiram and ethyl alcohol was observed by chance in 1937, and the drug was first used clinically in 1948. The early enthusiasm for the drug was based on clinical reports and poorly controlled research studies. A more measured attitude has followed better designed research in more recent years. Nevertheless, most authorities would accept that disulfiram has a role to play in the treatment of alcohol problems.

Disulfiram works by inhibiting the action of liver enzymes responsible for the breakdown of acetaldehyde, the principal metabolic product of ethyl alcohol. Acetaldehyde is a toxic substance and its accumulation results in a disulfiram–ethanol reaction. This is characterized by some or all of the following symptoms: flushing, tachycardia, dizziness, nausea, vomiting, difficulty in breathing, headache and hypotension. The severity of the reaction depends on the doses of both alcohol and disulfiram but the reaction can be fatal. Great care should obviously be taken in prescribing disulfiram. The potential for reaction appears to last for 4–7 days after ingestion of disulfiram, but the manufacturers recommend that no alcohol should be taken for two weeks *(120)*.

Disulfiram treatment has a substantial list of contraindications. In view of the potentially severe nature of the disulfiram–ethanol reaction, clients with cardiovascular diseases, severe lung disease or chronic kidney disease should be excluded. Cardiovascular diseases are the main exclusion criterion. Other contraindications include idiopathic seizure disorder, pregnancy and a variety of psychiatric disorders. Disulfiram causes drowsiness and should not be prescribed to people whose risk of accidents at work would be increased. Fuller *(120)* discusses all these and other contraindications. The initial side effects include impotence, headache, fatigue, dermatitis, gastritis and a metallic or garlic-like taste, but these largely disappear spontaneously or after adjustment of dosage. Moreover, one should be wary of possible interactions with other drugs *(120)*, and peripheral neuropathy is a common problem from long-term use (over six months).

Fuller *(120)* states that disulfiram is particularly suited to middle-aged problem drinkers with some degree of social stability and without significant depression. This conclusion is based on research data that do not cover women. In his practice, Fuller restricts the use of disulfiram to the clients of total abstinence programmes who have relapsed to drinking. Brewer *(121)* has claimed successful results with the use of disulfiram linked to probation for men with repeated drunkenness offences, a group that would conventionally be considered to have a poor prognosis. Others *(120)* have questioned the ethical propriety of this coercive use of disulfiram (see also Chapter 14). It would seem sensible to reserve disulfiram for people who are ready to change their drinking behaviour, and to exclude those who do not recognize a problem (those in the contemplation or precontemplation stages of change) on the grounds that such clients may drink while disulfiram is active.

Fuller *(120)* discusses the clinical issues in disulfiram treatment, which need not be considered in any detail here. Brewer *(122)* has argued that the standard dose of 250 mg disulfiram is often inadequate to produce the disulfiram–ethanol reaction, and that doses of up to 500 mg do not result in significant adverse effects. Fuller *(120)* has disputed this and it remains a contentious issue. There is no doubt, however, that different clients need different dosages, which must be individually adjusted.

Effectiveness

There are two forms of disulfiram administration at present – oral and implant. In the traditional use of disulfiram, it is prescribed to clients to take orally at home. This unsupervised use of disulfiram has limited evidence of effectiveness. In a well designed study, Fuller and his colleagues *(123,124)* found that clients instructed to take either a standard regimen or an inactive dose of disulfiram took longer to relapse than those in a control group that was given riboflavin. A large multicentre trial using the same design *(125)* did not replicate these results, but discovered that older, more socially stable men with good compliance in the standard regimen group reported fewer drinking days in the follow-up period than similar clients in control groups.

Fuller et al. *(125)* attributed these largely negative results to poor compliance, and it has long been clear that compliance is the major problem with disulfiram treatment. This has aroused much interest in the supervised use of disulfiram, for which there is stronger evidence of effectiveness *(126,127)*.

For example, Azrin et al. *(128)* reported that supervised disulfiram use combined with a community reinforcement programme (see

Chapter 10) was considerably more effective than traditional, unsupervised disulfiram among male drinkers with severe problems. For married clients, supervised disulfiram alone gave optimal results, suggesting a clear matching strategy based on the client's marital status. The only limitation of this study was a small sample size, and the comparison needs to be repeated with a larger sample. An accumulation of other evidence, however, also supports the supervised use of disulfiram, particularly for the types of client normally considered to have a poor prognosis, such as those habitually committing drunkenness offences, those with a concurrent heroin addiction and those with a history of repeated treatment failure *(127)*. In a multicentre trial, Chick et al. *(129)* found that supervised disulfiram use was superior to supervised administration of vitamin C on a range of outcome measures.

A professional (a physician, nurse, counsellor, social worker or probation officer) or a close relative of the client, usually the spouse, can provide supervision. Although supervised administration of disulfiram is recommended, it is not without problems and must be done sensitively. If not, the experience can be demeaning for the client and can create conflict between spouses. For this reason, supervision by a clinic staff member or some other neutral person is often preferable. If done by a spouse, supervision should be part of a contract detailing mutual rights and obligations, and should be seen unambiguously as a means of supporting the client, not as a method for checking up on him or her. In general, supervision should be seen as only one aspect of the wider issue of encouraging and monitoring compliance with taking disulfiram *(127)*.

An earlier response to the problem of compliance was to try surgical implants in subcutaneous tissue from which disulfiram is gradually released. Mattick & Jarvis *(5)* have reviewed the results of controlled research on these implants, concluding that the procedure appears to have only a small effect on drinking behaviour beyond the placebo effects of surgery. Moreover, implants have a number of disadvantages that affect their use. First, the widespread use of surgery is clearly more difficult than oral administration. Second, surgery carries some risks and the implant is effective only for a limited time, after which surgery needs to be repeated. Third, there is considerable doubt as to whether surgical implants can provide levels of circulating disulfiram adequate to produce the disulfiram–ethanol reaction following alcohol consumption *(130)*.

Effects on Drinking Behaviour

Disulfiram treatment is not a type of aversion therapy (see Chapter 10), and classical (Pavlovian) conditioning is unlikely to play much of a part in its effects on drinking behaviour. This is shown by the fact that disulfiram can be effective without the client ever experiencing a reaction. In the earlier use of disulfiram, a challenge dose combined with alcohol was routinely given to demonstrate to the client what would happen if he or she attempted to drink outside the clinic. Nowadays, however, giving clients a vivid description of the reaction and stern warnings about the consequences of drinking is thought preferable and entirely adequate *(120)*.

Given the evidence that the deterrent effects of disulfiram, not its pharmacological effects, are responsible for changing drinking behaviour, disulfiram treatment should properly be seen as a type of instrumental (operant) conditioning and as a form of contingency management (see Chapter 10). In other words, disulfiram affects behaviour by altering the consequences of drinking. For the problem drinker, alcohol consumption normally involves delayed negative consequences (or punishment) that have less influence on behaviour than the immediate gratification. Disulfiram replaces delayed with immediate negative consequences. The drinker's awareness of these changed contingencies is crucial to the success of the treatment. From this point of view, disulfiram is not a medical treatment at all but a form of behaviour therapy; a respectable argument could be mounted that it should not be included in the present chapter but in the next *(126)*.

The question then arises as to what happens when the changed contingencies are no longer present – in other words, when the client stops taking disulfiram. Has the client learned anything? Brewer *(131)* has suggested that disulfiram treatment involves a naturalistic form of cue exposure with response prevention (see Chapter 10). The client on disulfiram is exposed to mood states and external situations that would normally involve a high risk of excessive drinking, but is restrained by the knowledge of what would follow if drinking took place. By this means, the high-risk situations lose their potency to provoke excessive drinking. This idea has some theoretical problems, but is an interesting suggestion that should be researched. What can be concluded, however, is that attention should be paid during disulfiram treatment to the acquisition of skills and behaviour that will assist the client to avoid relapse afterwards (see Chapter 11).

Place in the Range of Available Treatment Options

As stated at the beginning of this section, disulfiram certainly has a role in a modern treatment service but this role is likely to be limited by a number of factors. The first is the long list of contraindications that exclude a significant proportion of clients. Confining disulfiram to those for whom research evidence of effectiveness exists *(120)* excludes many more, including clients who are young, female, depressed or socially unstable, and those who have successfully maintained total abstinence without the drug. Second, disulfiram seems to be unacceptable to about half of a typical clientele *(5)*. If the overriding principle of client choice is adopted (see Chapter 4), less than half may choose disulfiram.

As we have seen, the evidence indicates that supervised use is best, and some clients may find supervision unacceptable or lack a suitable supervisor. In addition, supervision may be contraindicated, as discussed above. Because of the evidence reviewed, disulfiram implants are not recommended for clinical use, except possibly in life-threatening circumstances where other means of persuading the client to stop drinking are not viable.

Even when oral disulfiram is considered the treatment of choice, it should normally be combined with counselling or behaviour therapy in a multimodal programme *(120)*. Specific treatment packages in which disulfiram is combined with a behavioural approach are described in the next chapter. On the positive side, successful disulfiram treatment often provides the client with both a break from the harm caused by excessive drinking and the opportunity to reorder a chaotic life.

Other Deterrent Drugs

The main alternative to disulfiram is calcium carbimide citrate (CCC). There is far less evidence to judge its effectiveness and it is far less widely used than disulfiram, being unavailable, for example, in the United States. CCC produces a reaction with ethanol by the same mechanism as disulfiram, but the two drugs show significant pharmacological differences. While disulfiram takes up to 12 hours to reach its full potential and remains active for several days, CCC can reach maximum effect within 1 hour but remains potent for only about 24 hours. Apart from an anti-thyroid effect (the reason for the ban in the United States), CCC appears to be relatively free of side effects *(120)*.

The more rapid onset and more severe reaction than that from disulfiram led Peachey et al. *(132)* to suggest that CCC could be used as part of a relapse prevention procedure when the client is unexpectedly faced with a high-risk situation for drinking; that is, as a kind of emergency kit. In a controlled trial of CCC, these authors could find no superiority to a placebo. Since most patients in both groups believed they were taking active medication throughout the study, the authors argued for a strong deterrent effect of CCC. Nevertheless, more research evidence of effectiveness is clearly needed before CCC can be recommended for routine use in treatment.

Metronidazole is useful in the treatment of urinary and vaginal infections. It has also been reported to produce a taste aversion to alcohol and was therefore suggested as a deterrent agent. There is no evidence whatever of its effectiveness in treatment *(1)* and its use cannot be recommended.

EFFECT-ALTERING DRUGS

Drugs that alter the effects of alcohol have attracted a great deal of interest in recent years. They are intended to suppress drinking behaviour, presumably by blocking the reinforcing or intoxicating properties of alcohol at the neuronal synapses; they supposedly prevent the drinker from experiencing the rewarding effects of alcohol. In addition, these drugs are often claimed to reduce the desire for the effects of alcohol, and they are sometimes known as anticraving drugs.

Naltrexone

Naltrexone is the leading candidate in this class at the time of writing. It is an opioid antagonist and was originally developed for the treatment of heroin addiction. On the assumption that the neural reward pathways for alcohol were similar to those for opiates, naltrexone was tested in the treatment of alcohol dependence. Amid much publicity and promises of being a new wonder drug in the treatment of alcoholism, it was recently approved for use in the United States.

Volpicelli et al. *(133)* have used naltrexone combined with standard psychotherapy in a placebo-controlled, double-blind study of recently detoxified problem drinkers. The preliminary results suggested that the combined treatment resulted in lower levels of alcohol craving, fewer drinking days and lower rates of relapse compared with placebo. In an attempt to extend these findings, O'Malley et al. *(134)* randomly assigned clients to receive either naltrexone or a placebo, plus coping skills/relapse prevention therapy or supportive psychotherapy. At assessment following the twelve-week treatment phase of the study, naltrexone proved to be superior to the placebo on a range of measures of drinking and alcohol-related problems. The highest rates of abstinence were shown by people who had received both naltrexone and supportive psychotherapy. Among the clients who resumed drinking, however, those who had received naltrexone combined with coping skills therapy were least likely to have relapsed to excessive consumption. The main limitation of this study is that no follow-up results were published, but these are presumably forthcoming. Meanwhile, naltrexone seems a useful addition to treatment, at least for short-term benefits.

Serotonin Uptake Inhibitors

The emergence of serotonin uptake inhibitors as a possible treatment for alcohol problems is based on recent advances in the understanding of the neurochemical basis of alcohol dependence and, in particular, the involvement of neuronal pathways subserved by the neurotransmitter serotonin. These pathways are implicated in the sensations of hunger and satiety and in mood; according to abundant evidence from animal and human studies, the same pathways affect alcohol consumption and dependence *(135)*.

Drugs in this class inhibit uptake (or reuptake) of serotonin at neuronal synapses and thus increase serotonin transmission. Several randomized, double-blind, placebo-controlled trials with various serotonin uptake inhibitors (such as fluoxetine, citalopram, zimeldine and viqualine) have shown average short-term reductions in alcohol consumption of about 20% in heavy social drinkers and subjects with mild or moderate dependence who are not receiving other treatment or advice. The effects on drinking occur within a few days of administration and thus earlier than those on depression and other moods.

From the evidence of these trials, the side effects of serotonin uptake inhibitors are said to be mild and transient *(136)*. Zimeldine has been withdrawn from the market in the United States, however, because it resulted in influenza-like symptoms and neuropathy in a significant number of patients being treated for depression. The seriousness of the side effects produced by these drugs is thus unclear. Although side effects may limit compliance, serotonin uptake inhibitors are easily administered and require to be taken only once per day. Considerable doubt remains as to how they exert their effects on drinking – for example, by a general effect on appetitive behaviour or by a more specific alcohol-related mechanism *(137)*.

Naranjo et al. *(138)* recently reported the results of a study in which citalopram was combined with brief psychosocial intervention and compared with placebo plus psychosocial intervention among heavy drinkers recruited by newspaper advertisements. The authors confirmed the short-term effects on drinking behaviour reported in previous studies, but found no benefit from citalopram over a twelve-week treatment period. Although both groups reduced consumption, citalopram had no detectable effect at follow-up eight weeks after treatment termination. The authors speculate that tolerance to the effects of citalopram may have been responsible for the failure to find long-term benefits.

Despite this negative finding and other suggestions that the early promise of serotonin uptake inhibitors has not been realized, research is proceeding. These drugs may prove useful in the treatment of alcohol problems, particularly for clients with high levels of dependence and strong feelings of craving or for more impulsive clients. In addition, it has been suggested that they may be helpful in the treatment of alcohol-related cognitive impairment *(136)*. These potential applications need to be clearly confirmed in well controlled clinical trials with clients seeking treatment, however, before routine clinical use can be envisaged. Even then, serotonin uptake inhibitors would probably have a limited role in treatment.

Other Effect-altering Drugs

Other drugs are under investigation as possible pharmacotherapies for alcohol dependence. A dopamine agonist, bromocriptine, has been shown to reduce drinking in experimental animals but less so than the serotonin uptake inhibitors. One clinical trial has shown that bromocriptine reduces craving and improves social functioning in problem drinkers seeking treatment *(139)*. Another dopamine agonist, tiapride, has been reported to help clients stay abstinent, but samples have been confined to those with concomitant anxiety or depression *(140)*.

Drugs affecting other neurotransmitters and receptors have also been examined. Lhuintre et al. *(141)* reported that calcium bis acetyl homotaurine (a gamma-aminobutyric acid (GABA) receptor agonist) increased abstinence in clients with severe alcohol dependence. Samson et al. *(142)* reported that a partial inverse benzodiazepine agonist reduces alcohol consumption in rats and appears to work by preventing intoxication.

Other research has been done with acamprosate, whose mechanism of action is unknown. Randomized clinical trials have shown that it is acceptable to problem drinkers and has beneficial effects on abstinence rates *(143)*. The effects of lithium have also been explored but studies have found no therapeutic effect compared with a placebo *(144)*.

Of course, all these drugs are in the experimental stage and await firm evidence of clinical effectiveness. Their availability for research or treatment purposes varies from country to country.

PSYCHOTROPIC MEDICATIONS

Psychotropic or mood-altering drugs are used, as seen in Chapter 2, in the detoxification of people who are highly dependent on alcohol. They have also been investigated as agents that may decrease the desire to drink. They have one further use: the treatment of people who show both alcohol problems and clinically significant mood disorders. Here they are used to treat not alcohol problems *per se* but the associated psychopathology. It is important to recognize people with a dual diagnosis, who have a poor prognosis and are likely to drop out of treatment. One can reasonably assume that successful treatment of the psychiatric disorder would increase the chances of recovery from the alcohol problems.

Distinguishing cause from effect in problem drinkers with mood disorders, however, is often difficult. Clinical experience shows that apparent psychopathology often disappears relatively quickly after the attainment of abstinence or moderate drinking, and is therefore likely to be secondary to excessive drinking. For this reason, sufficient time must be allowed after detoxification to determine whether psychotropic medication is necessary. In other cases, any remaining psychiatric problems can be treated by non-pharmacological means, by behavioural or cognitive therapy. Great care should obviously be taken in the prescription of drugs that can produce dependence in people who are already dependent on alcohol, particularly problem drinkers who are also polydrug users. Nevertheless, psychotropic medication has a limited role in the treatment of alcohol problems.

Antidepressants

In many problem drinkers, depression is a reaction to the chaotic effects of alcohol dependence on their lives, and resolves itself if drinking stops or decreases. A rule of thumb is to allow at least three weeks after detoxification, after which tricyclic or other antidepressant medication can be considered if the depression persists *(5)*. The major exception is a severe depressive disorder with suicidal ideation; problem drinkers are well known to have a high risk of suicide. Even here the use of medication should be reconsidered after the depression has abated. There is certainly no evidence that antidepressants are effective with problem drinkers in general *(1)*.

Anxiolytics

Apart from their important role in detoxification, there is no convincing rationale for the use of benzodiazepines in the treatment of alcohol problems *(5)*, either for problem drinkers in general or for those showing evidence of significant anxiety. Indeed, given the abuse potential of benzodiazepines and the danger of cross-dependence, their use is contraindicated.

Problem drinkers often complain of anxiety after detoxification but this usually subsides in time. If separate treatment of anxiety is necessary, non-pharmacological means can be used (see Chapter 10). In addition, the non-benzodiazepine anxiolytic, buspirone, a drug with apparently low abuse potential and few other contraindications, has been suggested to be useful in the treatment of the problem drinkers who meet the criteria for generalized anxiety disorder *(145)*. Research on this is proceeding.

THE ROLE OF PHARMACOTHERAPY

Disulfiram, especially in supervised administration, has a part to play in the treatment of alcohol problems. Psychotropic medication has a limited role for certain clients in certain circumstances. A range of effect-altering drugs is under active study and, although clinical trials have been disappointing on the whole, may hold some promise for the future. Even where the usefulness of pharmacotherapy has been established, as with disulfiram and apparently naltrexone, however, the evidence clearly shows that drugs should be combined with cognitive–behavioural therapy or some other kind of psychosocial intervention. The conclusion, widely accepted by treatment providers and researchers, must be that pharmacological approaches are adjunctive rather than of central importance in the treatment of alcohol problems.

The evidence reviewed in this chapter warns against the expectation of finding a chemical cure for alcohol dependence. Although the popular media sometimes stoke such hopes, the many causes and dimensions of alcohol dependence and problems make it most unlikely that a single cure will ever be found; research and treatment must adjust to this reality.

10

Cognitive–behavioural Approaches

The treatment modalities described in this chapter include some of the most effective methods examined in the research literature. Some clients may well be better suited to cognitive–behavioural methods than others, and some should be directed to alternative forms of treatment. Nevertheless, on the whole, properly conducted research trials support cognitive–behavioural approaches more strongly than any other general type of treatment.

The cognitive–behavioural perspective on treatment is based on the assumption that problem drinking, like any other drinking, is mainly learned behaviour. Thus, the purpose of therapy is to unlearn destructive or maladaptive forms of drinking behaviour and replace them with healthier and better adapted patterns, including total abstinence when necessary. Particularly important is the idea that the way that people drink is heavily influenced by the beliefs and expectations about the effects of alcohol that they have learned in a sociocultural context; hence the cognitive aspect of the approaches. More basic forms of learning, such as classical and operant conditioning, however, are still very important in the cognitive–behavioural perspective. This chapter includes older forms of treatment, such as aversion therapy, that are based on a purely behavioural (related to conditioning) set of assumptions.

One should note that these assumptions about learning theory are by no means undermined by a belief in genetic influences on the variation in people's drinking. It is widely accepted that, no matter exactly how heredity contributes to problem drinking, the mechanism of this inheritance is very unlikely to be a single gene and much more likely to be a polygenic predisposition to heavy drinking or alcohol dependence. It is not even clear whether this mechanism is specific to alcohol or is a more general predisposition to deviant forms of behaviour. In any event, the form that drinking behaviour takes does not emerge in a social vacuum, but has to be learned in a specific cultural context. Thus the relevance of a learning theory account of problem drinking and a cognitive–behavioural approach to treatment is undiminished. Because something is partly inherited does not mean that it cannot be changed.

The rubric cognitive–behavioural covers a diverse range of methods. This gives broad scope for matching clients to different forms of treatment within this family of approaches. An important aspect of the cognitive–behavioural perspective on treatment is that the particular approach to each case should be determined by the different functions alcohol serves for the individual client. This is the basis of the so-called broad spectrum approach, which was developed in the 1970s. It is still a useful way of looking at treatment and is described later in this chapter. The fundamental principle, that treatment should be tailored to the needs of the individual, applies to all cognitive–behavioural therapy. A treatment programme for the individual client may well consist of a judicious combination of the methods described in this chapter.

Another crucial assumption of the cognitive–behavioural perspective is that performance-based methods are superior to word-based methods in producing desirable changes in behaviour. That is, treatment methods that ask clients to do something, and give them training and practice in new skills and specific coping behaviour, produce better results than methods that rely merely on the discussion of the client's problem and verbal persuasion, as in traditional psychotherapy and counselling methods. Evidence to support this assertion comes from comparative studies of treatment for both behavioural problems in general *(146)* and alcohol problems in particular *(51)*.

MARITAL AND FAMILY THERAPY

The client's spouse and other family members may be involved in treatment for several reasons. Problem drinkers often show significant marital and family problems. It is often unclear which comes first, but the two typically have a reciprocal relationship: the client's drinking makes family adjustment worse, which aggravates the drinking problem. There is also good evidence of a strong association between good family adjustment and the outcome of treatment for alcohol problems; family conflicts are a common reason for relapse, and the family can give invaluable support to the client during and after treatment. It follows that treatment methods that improve family relationships should also improve outcome.

The heading of marital and family therapy covers a number of different approaches, based on different theoretical perspectives. These include the following.

Behavioural family therapy is based on the social learning theory principles briefly described above. It uses specific techniques, such as behaviour contracting, communication skills training and behaviour rehearsal, to modify and support abstinence or moderate drinking.

Spouse therapy is directed towards the spouse and aims to provide supportive counselling or teach behavioural reinforcement strategies to strengthen the client's changed behaviour.

Systems family therapy is based on systems theory. It aims to explore the role of alcohol within the family system and to help family members work on aspects of relationships that are dynamically related to problem drinking.

Interactive couples' group therapy is based on the premise that spouses can improve their communication with each other by taking part in supportive group discussions with other couples having similar problems.

This chapter discusses only the first two of these methods, because of evidence that they are effective treatment modalities. According to this evidence, behavioural family therapy produces superior results to either the systems or interactive approaches. Moreover, although including other family members in the treatment process may well be beneficial, the available evidence relates entirely to behavioural marital therapy. Descriptions of marital or family systems therapy *(99,147)* and interactive couples' groups *(148)* may be found elsewhere.

Behavioural Marital Therapy

O'Farrell *(149)* describes a behavioural marital therapy programme that involves couples' groups. The programme begins with sessions with each couple that aim to establish a therapeutic relationship and allow a careful assessment of drinking and the marital relationship. An important part of the programme is the use of disulfiram supervised by the spouse (see Chapter 9) and the therapist helps to negotiate a behavioural contract between client and spouse. O'Farrell *(149)* describes the structure and procedures of behavioural marital therapy in detail; they include methods to increase shared rewarding activities and training in communication and negotiation skills. They also include ways of dealing with obstacles to progress, such as alcohol-related crises, potentially violent relationships and non-compliance with various aspects of the programme. At the end of the programme, periodic follow-up contacts are arranged to help maintain progress.

Noel & McCrady *(150)* describe an alternative form of behavioural marital therapy that does not involve disulfiram. This incorporates three components: a behavioural alcohol treatment programme for the client, interventions focusing on the spouse's behaviour as it directly relates to the client's drinking, and behavioural marital therapy on a conjoint basis. The last component contains many of the specific techniques included in the O'Farrell programme *(149)*.

Evidence of Effectiveness

Miller & Hester *(1)* and Mattick & Jarvis *(5)* review the evidence for the effectiveness of marital and family therapy in general. McCrady et al. *(151)* report evidence specifically in favour of behavioural marital therapy from a study of varying degrees of spouse involvement in therapy. This found that problem drinkers given behavioural marital therapy – the highest level of spouse involvement – showed more rapid reductions in drinking and better maintenance of abstinence than two control groups. Further, marriages remained more stable and marital satisfaction was higher in the group receiving behavioural marital therapy. The advantage in drinking outcomes was maintained at follow-up after 18 months *(152)*.

Similarly, O'Farrell et al. *(153)* report that, in comparison to a group given interactive couples' therapy and a group receiving individual counselling, problem drinkers who received behavioural marital therapy showed superior scores on an index of overall drinking outcomes, as well as greater improvement on a range of measures of the quality of the marriage. The authors explain this difference by the programme's inclusion of performance-based learning of new skills and supervised disulfiram use. At a two-year follow-up *(154)* behavioural marital therapy was no longer superior to the other two groups on drinking outcome measures, but clients who had received either kind of couples' therapy showed evidence of somewhat better marital adjustment than those who had received individual counselling.

Finally, Bowers & Al-Redha *(155)* reported very positive results, compared with individual counselling, for what they describe as interactive couples' group therapy. Since this treatment programme included communication skills training, modelling and role playing, however, regarding it as a form of behavioural marital therapy seems legitimate.

Matching with Clients

Clearly, behavioural marital therapy can only be applied to clients who are married or in a relatively long-term relationship, which immediately excludes a large proportion of problem drinkers. On the other hand, O'Farrell & Cowles *(156)* argue that behavioural marital therapy should not be reserved for couples with serious marital difficulties, and that those with low or moderate difficulties can work together to achieve agreed goals. In the case of severely damaged relationships, special modifications of the treatment method may be necessary that involve more individual attention. Nevertheless, it appears sensible to concentrate the use of behavioural marital therapy on clients whose drinking problem and marital relationship seem to be linked.

The Institute of Medicine *(3)* has described a matching strategy for marital therapy. This involves the client's endorsement of the special goals of marital therapy, a low score on a scale of marital satisfaction and a reasonable likelihood of sustaining attendance at treatment sessions, as shown by a high social stability rating and the willingness of the spouse to participate.

Spouse Therapy

The stages of change model (Chapter 8) is as relevant to family and marital therapy as to any other treatment approach *(157)*. In particular, spouse therapy can be used in the contemplation or precontemplation stages, when the problem drinker is either undecided and inconsistent about whether a problem exists or flatly refuses to admit a problem with alcohol. In practice, this means that the involvement of the spouse can be used to encourage the client to seek treatment or to maintain his or her commitment once treatment has begun.

Research has found that receiving behavioural marital therapy appeared to prevent dropping out of treatment, and this was suggested to be due to the involvement of the spouse in the treatment process *(158)*. As to the initiation of treatment, Sisson & Azrin *(159)* reported on the effects of a programme designed to teach family members (usually wives) behavioural contingency skills for coping with problem drinkers. This reinforcement programme resulted in the entry into treatment of significantly more problem drinkers than did a more traditional programme consisting of alcohol education, individual supportive counselling for the spouse and referral to Alanon (the self-help fellowship for spouses of members of AA). Moreover, the problem drinkers with relatives in the reinforcement programme showed a significantly lower level of alcohol consumption before entering treatment. Sisson & Azrin *(160)* have described the reinforcement method in detail. Several other studies have demonstrated the benefits of spouse or family member involvement to the initiation or maintenance of treatment *(5,156)*.

THE COMMUNITY REINFORCEMENT APPROACH

The community reinforcement approach is one of the most successful treatment programmes described in the literature. The full approach consists of a broad range of treatment components that all have the aim of engineering the client's social environment (including the family and work environments) so that sobriety is rewarded and intoxication unrewarded. Although based firmly on the traditional principles of instrumental learning, the modern form of the community reinforcement approach includes methods to change clients' beliefs and expectations, and it is therefore appropriately placed under the general heading of cognitive–behavioural therapy.

Hunt & Azrin *(161)* originally developed the community reinforcement approach for use with inpatients. Over the years, it has been modified for use with outpatients, and supervised disulfiram use (see Chapter 9) has played an increasingly critical role in its success. Nevertheless, clients for whom disulfiram is contraindicated or those who refuse it can still benefit from the community reinforcement approach. The type of spouse therapy described in the previous section *(156)* is an important adjunct of the approach.

Components

As described by Sisson & Azrin *(162),* the full community reinforcement approach consists of seven components:

1. a prescription for disulfiram;
2. the monitoring of disulfiram ingestion by a significant other person;
3. reciprocal marriage counselling, not unlike behavioural marital therapy described in the previous section;
4. job finding;
5. social skills training;
6. advice on social and recreational activities; and
7. assistance with controlling the urge to drink.

Sisson & Azrin *(162)* emphasize that the community reinforcement approach is a very intensive form of treatment involving rapid intervention in a wide range of life activities, typically over a period of 4–6 weeks. Many components of the programme should be implemented quickly to give the client an immediate experience of success and the rewards of sobriety. Thus, the client should first be seen the same day or next day after meeting the decision to obtain help, and the disulfiram regime should commence straight away.

Sisson & Azrin *(162)* give details on implementing the community reinforcement approach. The full programme includes the setting-up of a job finding club in which clients are given practical guidance on how to find a job, training in interviewing skills and other relevant assistance. A "united club" is also established to enable clients to find social support, develop non-drinking friendships and have an enjoyable time without alcohol. Social and recreational counselling in respect of non-drinking activities is provided. When resources are available, the client receives financial assistance to obtain a place to live, a telephone, subscriptions to magazines and a driving licence. For many socially isolated clients, the social network must be recreated from scratch and this can be assisted by a "buddy system", in which a successful former client befriends a new client and provides the monitoring of disulfiram that is considered essential to the programme.

Suitable Clients

In principle, the community reinforcement approach is suitable for all problem drinkers, particularly those with serious problems, among whom it has proved much more successful than many other treatment approaches. Clearly, however, the full community reinforcement approach is not appropriate for all clients. The marriage counselling component is suitable only for those in a regular relationship, and the job finding component for those who are unemployed. (Moreover, the potential success of job finding varies according to the rate of unemployment in the country in question.) In addition, the full programme is relatively expensive and time-consuming; it may be beyond the resources of many agencies. The question of its cost–effectiveness in comparison with other methods must be borne in mind (see Chapter 13).

At the very least, however, the principles of the approach (behaviour contracting, contingency management and, in general, the attempt to change the social environment so that sobriety is reinforced and heavy drinking not reinforced) may be applied with suitable modifications to each case. The community reinforcement approach has proved especially impressive with socially unstable and isolated clients with a poor prognosis for traditional forms of treatment, including those who have failed in treatment several times in the past.

Evidence of Effectiveness

The community reinforcement approach has been evaluated with impressively positive results in several studies. In the original evaluation, Hunt & Azrin *(161)* tested the effectiveness of the approach when added to an inpatient programme and compared with a traditional mixture of alcohol education and AA. At follow-up after six months, clients who received the community reinforcement approach were drinking on an average of 14% of days, compared with 79% in the controls; the controls spent 12 times as many days unemployed and 15 times as many days in an institution as the experimental group.

Azrin *(163)* evaluated improvements in the community reinforcement approach, including the addition of a disulfiram component. At follow-up after six months, clients who received the community reinforcement approach showed fewer than 1% drinking days per month, compared with 55% in a control group that received a standard hospital programme. The two groups also showed very large differences in days unemployed and days spent away from home. Working with outpatients, Mallams et al. *(164)* evaluated one component of the community reinforcement approach: the non-drinking social club. Clients encouraged to attend showed greater reductions in drinking, spent less time in settings used for heavy drinking and showed fewer behavioural problems than those not encouraged to attend.

Finally, Azrin et al. *(128)* compared the effectiveness of the full community reinforcement approach with just the disulfiram component, and compared disulfiram use with and without supervision. Table 5 shows the main results. Overall, the full community reinforcement approach programme obtained the best results, while the supervised disulfiram regime was superior to unsupervised disulfiram (see Chapter 9). In addition, the data indicated an interesting interaction. For single clients, disulfiram alone was ineffective and the addition of the community reinforcement approach led to a significant improvement in results; for married clients, the community reinforcement approach gave no additional benefit, since they had already reached the maximum number of days of abstinence through supervised disulfiram use. This finding makes sense if it is assumed that a partner is necessary for successful supervised disulfiram treatment, and that married clients already have access to many of the reinforcements provided by the community reinforcement approach. This study examined a small sample but suggests a matching strategy, reserving the full community reinforcement approach for single clients.

Table 5. Mean number of days of abstinence during 30 days before interview for married and single clients

Treatment	Days of abstinence	
	Single clients	Married clients
Unsupervised disulfiram use	6.8	17.4
Supervised disulfiram use	8.0	30.0
Supervised disulfiram use and community reinforcement approach	28.3	30.0

Source: adapted from Azrin et al. *(128)*. Reproduced by kind permission of Elsevier Science Ltd, The Boulevard, Langford Lane, Kidlington, OX5 1GB, United Kingdom.

THE BROAD SPECTRUM APPROACH

The basic assumption of this approach is that a functional analysis of an individual case of problem drinking reveals specific antecedents and consequences (or cues and reinforcements) of heavy drinking. In other words, drinking is functionally related to other issues in a person's life. To take a simple example, someone might drink heavily in every social situation because he or she has learned that alcohol reduces the anxiety that would otherwise appear. According to this view, a treatment programme that addresses a broad spectrum of problems in living and is specially adjusted to suit the needs of the individual client is more likely to succeed than one that concentrates only on drinking.

In principle, a large number of treatment techniques and methods could form part of the broad spectrum approach; indeed, all the methods mentioned in this chapter would qualify. Several methods addressing particular skill deficits – such as training in social skills, problem solving and communication – are prominent in broad spectrum approaches. This section considers treatment methods aimed at negative emotional states and associated cognitions that are often linked to problem drinking.

Anxiety Management

One of the most common reasons that problem drinkers give for drinking too much is the need to reduce anxiety and cope with situations in which it arises. Reflecting this connection, anxiety disorders – single phobias, agoraphobia, generalized anxiety disorder and panic attacks – occur more frequently among problem drinkers than in the general population.

The situation is complicated by the fact that alcohol withdrawal symptoms typically include a strong element of anxiety, and anxiolytic medication comprises the most common type of treatment of withdrawal symptoms (see Chapter 2). For many clients, anxiety simply disappears when they are fully detoxified. As with the pharmacological treatment of depression in problem drinkers (see Chapter 9), two or three weeks should be allowed to elapse before it is decided whether treatment of an anxiety disorder is needed. Non-pharmacological treatment should normally be preferred, because it is far safer and shows good evidence of effectiveness.

Stockwell & Town *(165)* have described the main ingredients of the modern approach to anxiety management following alcohol withdrawal. These are:

- relaxation training or a similar procedure;
- systematic desensitization and other behavioural strategies;
- cognitive strategies designed to amend unhelpful beliefs, thoughts and images associated with anxiety; and

- lifestyle modification to reduce anxiety and stress.

Self-help guides are often useful in the treatment of anxiety. For social anxiety, social skills training, assertiveness training or a mixture of both can be used.

Evidence of Effectiveness

Evaluations of relaxation training among problem drinkers have produced conflicting results *(1)*. A study by Rosenberg *(166)*, who compared clients receiving biofeedback relaxation training with those in an alcohol education control group, suggests a possible reason. Having measured the clients' level of anxiety, Rosenberg found that those with high levels showed significantly greater reductions in alcohol consumption if they had received relaxation training, while no difference was found among those low on anxiety. This supports the use of an obvious matching strategy: offering relaxation training to clients with high levels of anxiety.

As to systematic desensitization, the evidence is again mixed, although two studies *(167,168)* have found clear advantages over other forms of treatment. The studies were aimed at all problem drinkers, however, and more consistent results might have been obtained had those with higher levels of anxiety been selected.

Anger Management

Another emotion commonly associated with heavy drinking is anger. Many problem drinkers have difficulty in managing and expressing anger without the aid of alcohol. Of course, anger can have both constructive and destructive consequences, but the latter typically predominate in problem drinkers. For selected clients, therefore, training in the management of anger is an important part of the treatment programme, especially if it is combined with assertiveness training. Monti et al. *(11)* provide guidelines on treatment methods for anger management.

No research appears to have specifically addressed the effectiveness of anger management among problem drinkers. This is a clear gap in the research base for cognitive–behavioural treatment approaches. The topic is included here for the sake of completeness in describing the broad spectrum approach.

Cognitive Restructuring

Another important target in a broad spectrum approach is the negative thoughts that often precede heavy drinking. These cognitions are associated with feelings of low self-esteem, failure, helplessness and depression, and are a potent trigger for alcohol craving in many clients. Such thoughts (or self-talk) are typically automatic; the client is unaware of the link they provide between external events and the desire for alcohol effects. Moreover, they often act as a self-fulfilling prophecy: although they may be incorrect interpretations of events in the person's life, they have the effect of making these interpretations come true. To take an obvious example, people who believe that no one likes them are less likely to be able to make friends.

Cognitive restructuring comprises a family of techniques designed to help clients recognize and change the thoughts and feelings that lead to destructive drinking. It is based on the work of Beck et al. *(169)* on cognitive therapy for depression, and the principles of rational emotive therapy as developed by Ellis et al. *(170)*. The specific aims of cognitive restructuring are to enable the client:

1. to identify negative thoughts, particularly those automatic thoughts of which he or she was previously unaware, and to challenge them by familiarity with some of the main categories of irrational thinking as listed, for example, by Ellis & Harper *(171)*;

2. to interrupt the chain of thought that has led in the past to the desire for intoxication, possibly using the technique known as thought-stopping; and

3. to replace negative thoughts with more realistic, positive cognitions, which can be learned from modelling in group situations and role play (behavioural rehearsal) and carried out through the technique of self-talk modification *(172)*.

Monti et al. *(11)* and Jarvis et al. *(14)* provide more details on cognitive restructuring. Although cognitive restructuring is presented here as an approach to clients whose drinking pattern has been assessed as being strongly linked to negative thoughts, it can and should be used, as appropriate and in combination with other techniques, with everyone who receives a cognitive–behavioural form of treatment.

Evidence of Effectiveness

Jackson & Oei *(173)* compared cognitive restructuring with social skills training and a control condition of traditional supportive therapy. Immediately after treatment and at follow-up three months later, both cognitive–behavioural treatment groups were superior to the control group on a range of measures, including alcohol intake. In a larger study with longer follow-up, Oei & Jackson *(174)* compared groups given cognitive restructuring, social skills training or a combination of both with a control group given traditional supportive therapy. All three cognitive–behavioural groups were superior to the controls, on both drinking and social skill measures, for up to one year after treatment. The two groups given cognitive restructuring, however, continued to improve during the follow-up period and showed a better outcome at one-year follow-up than the group receiving social skills training alone. The group receiving a combination of cognitive restructuring and social skills training showed the best results.

Brandsma et al. *(175)* caried out a study to demonstrate the effectiveness of cognitive restructuring in the form of rational behaviour therapy. Clients who received such therapy, either from professionals or in a self-help context, had a better drinking outcome at follow-up after 16 months than a control group receiving no treatment.

SKILLS TRAINING

Again, the methods described in this section are continuous with those of the last section (and, to some extent, with all the ingredients of the cognitive–behavioural approach to treatment). Both sets often complement each other in the best therapy programme for an individual client.

Skills training embraces a variety of methods with a common base in social learning theory *(176)*. This treatment perspective is sometimes known as the coping skills approach. It views alcohol problems and dependence as consequences of maladaptive, habitual responses to stresses and life problems. The assumption is that the individual has learned to cope with stressors by excessive drinking and that this has created a vicious circle of increasing drinking in response to increasing difficulties in living. The object of treatment is therefore to identify clients' particular coping deficits, and provide them with ways of coping that do not involve heavy drinking.

Social Skills

A major category of stress for problem drinkers and for many other people arises from the demands of relationships with other people. While not all problem drinkers are deficient in social skills, the need to reduce social anxiety is a common reason for heavy drinking. Hence the importance of social skills training in the range of cognitive–behavioural techniques on offer to problem drinkers.

Chaney *(177)* and Monti et al. *(11)* have described social skills training programmes. Social skills are seen as a combination of behavioural, affective and cognitive responses to environmental conditions. The microskills that might typically be targeted in a training programme include expressing emotion, effective listening, responding to criticism, refusing unreasonable requests, initiating conversations, nonverbal expression (such as eye contact) and giving and receiving compliments. Social skills training merges with what is conventionally known as assertiveness training, which involves helping clients communicate their feelings more directly and openly, thereby deriving more satisfaction and less frustration from relationships. In addition, the techniques of communication skills training, which was mentioned in connection with behavioural marital therapy, are a central aspect of social skills training. For this reason, these two are not considered under separate headings; guides to both may be found in Jarvis et al. *(14)*. Two other types of skill – problem solving and drink refusal – are considered separately below, although they, too, are often integral parts of social skills training.

Techniques often used in social skills training include therapist modelling (in which the therapist demonstrates desirable responses), behaviour rehearsal (role play) and feedback on the appropriateness of new behaviour from video recordings or other members of a therapy group. The group setting is normally preferred for social skills training for the very good reason that the skills to be improved are interpersonal in nature; the group provides a realistic setting in which to practise them and obtain useful feedback. Homework assignments, in which the client experiments with new responses in real-life situations, are also essential. As implied in the section on cognitive restructuring, clients may need to be taught alternative ways of thinking, as well as new ways of behaving, to counter self-defeating beliefs and attitudes. The assessment of specific skill deficits is an essential guide to the contents of social skills training for each client, and the method known as the situational competency test *(177)* may be used for this purpose (see Chapter 3).

Evidence of Effectiveness

Social skills training is one of the best supported treatment methods in the field of alcohol problems. Holder et al. *(4)* list 10 separate evaluations of social skills training that have reached positive conclusions as to its effectiveness, with no published studies reporting negative conclusions. Social skills training achieves the highest score on a weighted evidence index devised by these authors, which takes account of the balance between positive and negative findings among adequately designed studies. As space is limited, only a few of the more prominent studies are mentioned here.

In an influential study, Chaney et al. *(51)* investigated the effects of three abstinence-oriented treatment methods. One group received social skills training, which involved practice in responding to social situations that had been assessed as having a high risk of drinking for the clients. This was compared with another condition in which the same situations were the focus of group discussions with no behavioural intervention, and a third that involved standard hospital treatment. At follow-up after 12 months, the group with social skills training was clearly superior on a number of measures of drinking to the other two groups; the latter did not differ from each other. Jones et al. *(178)* partly replicated this finding, finding that both social skills training and group discussions of high-risk situations were better than standard treatment. The low rate of successful contact at follow-up may have prevented social skills training from emerging as superior.

Oei & Jackson *(179)* examined social skills training conducted in a group or on an individual basis. These two conditions were compared with traditional supportive therapy on a group or individual basis. Both of the groups receiving social skills training improved significantly more than the two others throughout a twelve-month follow-up period, but the two forms of social skills training showed no significant differences. Clearly, however, the group setting would have been much more cost-effective than the individual regime (see Chapter 13).

The studies above examined problem drinkers in general. Ferrell & Galassi *(180)* appear to have conducted the only study of clients who had been specially selected for their poor social skills. The results showed a clear superiority of an assertiveness training group over a discussion group at follow-up over a two-year period. Thus, although social skills training appears to be effective with the generality of clients with problem drinking, matching this form of skills training to those who seem to need it most may have additional advantages.

In the most recent major study of social skills training, Monti et al. *(181)* compared three social learning approaches to the treatment of problem drinking: communication skills training in groups or with the involvement of a spouse or other family member, and cognitive–behavioural mood management training in groups. At follow-up after six months, clients in both groups receiving communication skills training were drinking less than those in the mood management group.

Problem-solving Skills

As indicated above, training in problem-solving skills is similar in several ways to social skills training. It is often included under this rubric because the problems that the skills training method is designed to help solve are typically interpersonal. Nevertheless, the two types of training differ sufficiently in orientation and theoretical foundations for problem-solving skills to be considered separately.

Training in problem-solving skills is usually based on the theoretical analysis and method described by D'Zurilla & Goldfried *(182)*. The method is intended to help the client to generate and practise realistic alternative coping strategies and behaviour in response to situations involving a high risk of drinking. It consists of five well defined stages: orientation, definition, generation of alternatives, decision-making and verification. In other words, the client is helped:

- to define what exactly the problem is
- to imagine options for dealing with it
- to choose the best and most practical option
- to develop a detailed plan of action
- to put this plan into effect
- to evaluate the results in order to revise the plan if necessary.

Training can be given to either groups or individuals. The assumption is made that, following intensive training, the client can apply the method to deal with novel situations and problems. Monti et al. *(11)* and Jarvis et al. *(14)* provide guidance on the use of the method in the alcohol problems field.

Evidence of Effectiveness

The study by Chaney et al. *(51)* provides good evidence of the effectiveness of training in problem-solving skills; it formed an essential ingredient in a highly effective treatment method. No study, however, appears to have compared problem-solving skills training on its own with other varieties of the skills training approach.

Drink Refusal Skills

Compared with the other types of skills training in this section, training to refuse drinks may seem a rather narrow area. There are grounds, however, for believing that it is a highly specific and useful skill that problem drinkers can readily acquire. The problem drinker who is trying to abstain or drink moderately often encounters intense pressure to drink when he or she has decided not to do so. This is especially true for male clients who have tended to do their drinking in groups of men and who live in societies with unwritten but powerful rules on buying and accepting offered drinks. Training in drink refusal skills teaches clients how to refuse offers to drink with confidence and without giving offence. Monti et al. *(11)* and Jarvis et al. *(14)* provide guidance.

As with problem-solving skills training, no research appears to have evaluated the effects of drink refusal skills training in isolation, but it forms a part of the treatment packages found effective in several studies *(51,128)*.

Other Skills

A number of other microskills could be included under the heading of the skills training approach, but space prohibits detailed descriptions here. Monti et al. *(11)* cover this topic, dividing the skills into interpersonal and intrapersonal categories.

Contraindications for Skills Training

A wide range of problem drinkers can benefit from the skills training approach and many are likely to select it as a preferred treatment option. In two related circumstances, however, this approach is liable to be ineffective. Both concern the client's cognitive and intellectual ability to profit from skills training, which requires that the client be able to learn and remember new information and to use new behavioural skills.

First, a high proportion of problem drinkers, especially those with high levels of dependence and associated consumption, are cognitively impaired prior to and immediately after detoxification. This impairment includes many of the intellectual functions, such as abstraction and concept formation, that are necessary for the efficient absorption of skills training. Thus, some period of abstinence after detoxification may be necessary before applying the skills approach *(178)*. Neuropsychological tests (see Chapter 3) can be used to determine whether cognitive functioning has recovered sufficiently to allow treatment to begin.

Second, some problem drinkers have permanent or long-lasting cognitive impairment as a consequence of their drinking. This subgroup may not be able to benefit from skills training, especially if it contains a prominent cognitive component. Sanchez-Craig & Walker *(183)* compared coping skills training with covert sensitization (discussed below) and a discussion control group among "chronic alcoholics" in a halfway house. They found no benefit from coping skills training during a follow-up period of 18 months, and an interim assessment at 1 month after treatment showed that these clients had retained little of the content of the skills intervention.

The results of a study by Cooney et al. *(184)* bear out the suggestion that cognitively impaired clients should not be referred for skills training. These authors set out to test various matching hypotheses (see Chapter 4) in the context of a comparison between coping skills training and interactive group therapy given after inpatient treatment. The study provided good evidence for the usefulness of matching procedures with respect to sociopathy and global psychopathology. The researchers, however, had also predicted that cognitively impaired clients would do poorly with interactional therapy because they would be unable to profit from the interpersonal experience, and would do better with the coping skills approach because of its higher degree of structure and more focused goals. The results at follow-up after two years showed the exact opposite of this hypothesis. Clients with cognitive impairment had a better outcome with interactive group therapy, and those without impairment had a better outcome with coping skills training. The authors speculate that the cognitively impaired clients found the agenda of the coping skills programme too intellectually demanding and derived greater support from the interactive groups.

BEHAVIOURAL SELF-CONTROL TRAINING

This treatment approach is sometimes called self-management training. Although the principles underlying the approach could in theory be applied to a treatment goal of either abstinence or moderation, in practice behavioural self-control training has become identified with the latter. While it is a comparatively recent development, it has been subjected to more controlled trials and other research evaluations than any other treatment method for alcohol problems. The evidence of its effectiveness with problem drinkers with less severe dependence and problems is overwhelmingly positive.

A typical programme of behavioural self-control training consists of six steps:

1. setting limits
2. self-monitoring
3. reducing the rate of consumption
4. identifying antecedents to heavy drinking
5. identifying alternatives to heavy drinking
6. self-reinforcement.

The first task is to set limits to the amount of alcohol that should be consumed. This applies to average consumption over a week, for example, and to the maximum number of drinks allowed at any single drinking session, bearing in mind gender, weight and other factors that contribute to blood alcohol concentration and hence to the degree of intoxication experienced. The therapist can negotiate with the client to arrive at sensible levels of consumption, and limits normally take account of the levels recommended for safe drinking by medical authorities in the country in question. Drinks should be measured in terms of standard units of alcohol, if these have been defined in the country in question, and this concept should be carefully explained to the client. Limits should include two or three days of complete abstinence per week.

Next, the client should be given self-monitoring cards and asked to fill them in, before taking each drink, with details of the date, time, place, alcohol content, drinking company and setting. Difficulties in doing this can be discussed. Self-monitoring is an essential preliminary step to the other ingredients of behavioural self-control training.

Third, the client should learn and practise ways of cutting down the rate of consumption. These include slowing drinking by taking smaller and less frequent sips, switching from stronger to weaker drinks, interspersing alcoholic drinks with non-alcoholic beverages and using drink refusal skills.

Fourth, using an analysis of past drinking and current self-monitoring, the client should identify internal and external antecedents to heavy drinking and alcohol-related problems. These may ude times, places, people and particularly moods. The client may ı avoid these antecedents or make special plans to reduce the lihood that they will result in heavy drinking. At the same time, ecedents to moderate drinking can be identified and drinking rules oorated to increase the frequency of moderate drinking episodes.

Fifth, the client can learn and practise ways of coping with high- drinking situations. Depending on individual circumstances, these y include some of the skills and procedures mentioned in the last sections of this chapter. In general, the client can take up or ıme behaviour that does not involve any drinking This very often olves a complete change in lifestyle. The client needs to under- ıd that such radical changes in behaviour are necessary for the -control training to succeed, especially with relatively higher els of alcohol dependence.

Sixth, the client should be helped to set up a reward system for successful performance of target behaviour, even a minor victory h as keeping to a drinking limit on one occasion or obeying a spe- c drinking rule. Rewards may be of a material nature, involve the ve participation of a partner or be purely mental, in the form of gratulatory self-talk. The client must be persuaded that this is not zy or childish but an effective way of encouraging desirable nges in behaviour. The client's spouse should not be involved in ishment or deciding to withhold rewards when targets are not met.

Hester & Miller *(185)* and Jarvis et al. *(14)* provide fuller details he theory and methods of behavioural self-control training. It can given to groups or individuals; both formats have advantages and ıdvantages. It can also be conveyed through self-help manuals. se may be used as an adjunct to formal treatment, given out after a f counselling session or distributed with little or no personal tact with helpers (see Chapter 6).

tching with Clients

ce behavioural self-control training is aimed at the goal of derate drinking, all the considerations reviewed in Chapter 5 for selection of the goal of treatment are relevant here. As mentioned, clients given behavioural self-control training are mainly those with low or medium alcohol dependence and problems, but those with more severe problems can be considered for this approach in special circumstances. Chief among these circumstances is a history of repeated failure with total abstinence programmes or a refusal to countenance abstinence as a goal. In the latter case, the therapist should not turn the client away with instructions to return only when he or she accepts the need for abstinence. Rather, the therapist should actively help the client to attain the goal of moderation, even if highly doubtful about the wisdom of this course. Goals can always be reviewed in the light of subsequent experience.

Sanchez-Craig et al. *(186)* examined the results of a comparison of abstinence and moderation goals attached to the same form of behavioural skills training programme for low-dependence problem drinkers. The authors concluded that moderate drinking was the more appropriate goal because it was more acceptable to the majority of clients, and because most of those assigned to the goal of abstinence achieved a moderate drinking outcome on their own. Sanchez-Craig & Lei *(187)* further concluded that imposing the abstinence goal on the heavy-drinking clients in their sample was ineffective in promoting abstinence and counterproductive in encouraging moderation. A particular subgroup for which behavioural self-control training has proved effective comprises people who have been convicted of drink-driving offences *(1)*. The imposition of an abstinence goal is likely to be counterproductive with most such offenders.

The declared goal of treatment may have little to do with the final outcome. Many clients of abstinence programmes achieve moderation outcomes without specialized help; similarly, it is not uncommon to find that ex-clients of behavioural self-control training programmes have chosen and maintained a way of life without alcohol *(185)*. The role of treatment in this case may be to reduce the importance of drinking in the client's lifestyle to the point at which it is no longer seen as necessary to normal functioning.

In addition, in focusing on clients with less severe problems, behavioural self-control training is an essential element in broadening the base of treatment. Condensed forms of behavioural self-control training are one prominent form of the brief interventions that are described in Chapter 7 and aimed at the population of excessive drinkers not seeking help. Likewise, more extended forms of behavioural self-control training offered by specialist clinics are consistent with the aims of early intervention and secondary prevention.

Evidence of Effectiveness

As mentioned, considerable research on behavioural self-control training has yielded very encouraging results. Holder et al. *(4)* list 10 independent studies that found a significant superiority for behavioural self-control training over various control conditions. Depending on how behavioural self-control training is defined, the total number of such studies is likely to be somewhat greater. Most of these studies were well designed, with randomized control groups, blind follow-up and independent confirmation of clients' self-reports of progress. Against this, five studies failed to find a benefit of behavioural self-control training, but these were conducted mainly on drinkers with more severe problems.

Aggregating the results from a series of studies of behavioural self-control training, Miller & Baca *(188)* calculated that 60–70% of treated problem drinkers showed clear improvement on pre-treatment status at follow-up interviews up to two years after treatment. Follow-up ranging up to eight years after treatment showed an increasing proportion of clients becoming totally abstinent and a consistent 10–15% able to sustain moderate drinking with no alcohol-related problems *(185)*.

AVERSION THERAPIES

The category of aversion therapies includes the oldest applications of behavioural treatment in the field of alcohol problems. Therapy with nausea induced by emetine was used extensively in the United States during the 1940s, with very encouraging reported success rates. The reports in question, however, were all uncontrolled studies using clients with good prognoses for any form of treatment. When this therapy was subjected to controlled evaluation, the results were far less impressive.

All aversion therapies aim to reduce the client's desire for alcohol by using classical counter-conditioning techniques. They pair stimuli such as the sight, smell and taste of alcohol with one of a variety of unpleasant experiences. If successful, this method results in the client's acquiring a conditioned aversive response to alcohol and a resulting decrease in the desire to drink. As well as straightforward counter-conditioning, escape and avoidance conditioning paradigms have been used. Aversion therapies must be clearly distinguished from the use of deterrent drugs, which is based on entirely different principles (see Chapter 9).

Types

The four types of aversion therapy use different unpleasant experiences: nausea, electric shock, apnoea and unpleasant images. After early enthusiasm for chemical, nausea-based methods had subsided somewhat, electrical aversion methods began to be used because they were less arduous, and offered more control over the timing and severity of the aversive experience. It has been argued, however, that nausea is a more natural aversive response to drinking than electrically induced pain, and often occurs, for example, following an episode of food poisoning.

A very radical form of aversion therapy tried out during the 1960s used an injection of suxamethonium chloride to produce total paralysis of breathing and movement for about one minute. Research has failed to demonstrate any benefit from this form of treatment *(1)*, and this terrifying and dangerous procedure has no ethical justification whatever.

The fourth form of aversion therapy, covert sensitization, is discussed in more detail below.

Research

Research on aversion therapies represents one of the largest bodies of literature in the field of alcohol problems, but results are conflicting and confusing. There is some evidence that chemical aversion methods are superior to electrical methods in producing abstinence, and nausea-based methods (including motion-induced nausea) have been concluded to produce some short-term benefits *(12)*.

Nevertheless, chemical and electrical aversion methods have now been largely abandoned in most parts of the world. No matter what gains they are thought to produce, far more pleasant, less dangerous and less ethically problematic methods achieve at least as favourable results with less likelihood of treatment drop-out. These methods include many of those described in this chapter, and covert sensitization, which is the only form of aversion therapy that can currently be recommended.

Covert Sensitization

This method of aversion therapy is carried out entirely in the imagination. Unpleasant, usually nausea-provoking images are associated with alcohol and drinking behaviour. Thus in a typical procedure, the therapist asks and helps the client to visualize ordering a drink, bringing the glass to the lips and then drinking. At that moment, the client is asked to imagine an aversive stimulus, normally vomiting. This is repeated perhaps 20 times per session over the course of treatment, and supported by practice at home and in situations when the client feels the desire for a drink. Covert sensitization is obviously suited to an abstinence goal since it aims to produce an aversion to any alcohol.

Rimmele et al. *(189)* and Jarvis et al. *(14)* give further details of the method. The therapist should create five types of imaginary scene in collaboration with the client: drinking, aversion, relief, escape and avoidance. The therapist then uses the scenes as scripts, reading them to the client, who sits in a comfortable chair in a darkened room. Rimmele et al. *(189)* provide examples of all necessary types of script, as well as other procedural instructions. The best generalization from the clinic to the real environment is thought to be achieved when fantasies are closely tailored to the client's drinking preferences and personal aversions. For this reason, covert sensitization is recommended for use with individuals, not groups. A foul-smelling substance (valeric acid) has been used to help create nausea, with encouraging results *(190)*.

The exclusion criteria for covert sensitization are straightforward: present or past gastrointestinal disorders or heart disease, severe depression or suicidal ideation, and psychotic illness *(189)*. The therapist should take pains to ensure that the client does not perceive the method as a form of punishment for wrong-doing. Predicting who will do well with the method is difficult at the outset of treatment, but this may become clear after a few sessions. Elkins *(191)* showed that clients who are unable to experience conditioned nausea are less likely to benefit, and there are various ways of determining whether this is the case *(191)*. Such clients should be excluded and offered a different form of treatment, as should those who show any adverse reactions (such as nightmares). As ever, client choice should be an overriding consideration.

Evidence of Effectiveness

In the review by Holder et al. *(4)*, covert sensitization is the only form of aversion therapy to show a positive score on the weighted evidence index, with four studies showing favourable results and three failing to find a treatment effect. The negative studies may have been conducted in a group format or used incorrect conditioning procedures. Elkins *(191)* demonstrated that the strength of the conditioned aversive responses could predict the success of covert sensitization, and subsequent research has confirmed this *(189)*. Studies with carefully defined sensitization procedures and ways of documenting the establishment of conditioning have shown the most promising results.

CUE EXPOSURE

The last approach to be described in this chapter is also the newest, at least in terms of practical treatment delivery. Cue exposure is a promising method that requires more research support before it can be regarded as firmly established as an effective treatment for alcohol problems. Nevertheless, there is no reason to exclude it from a comprehensive treatment programme.

Like aversion therapy, cue exposure is founded on the principles of classical conditioning, although the consequences for treatment are very different. The general method of cue exposure has been used successfully in the treatment of phobias and other anxiety disorders and obsessive–compulsive disorders. Its application to alcohol dependence begins with the assumption that the craving for alcohol is linked to classically conditioned responses to alcohol-related stimuli that the client has frequently encountered during his or her drinking career. Such conditioned responses are thought to play a crucial role in the continuation of excessive drinking and to persist after extended periods of abstinence, thus making a crucial contribution to relapse following treatment. This is proposed as an explanation for the puzzling phenomenon whereby someone formerly dependent on alcohol experiences a sudden urge to drink after months or even years of abstinence. Particularly important among the stimuli that elicit this conditioned craving are internal mood states and the interoceptive effects of low doses of alcohol, which provoke a strong desire for more. In this way the theory also explains the phenomenon of loss of control over drinking *(192)*.

The aim of cue exposure is to expose the client to conditioned stimuli (or cues) that are relevant to his or her individual case in the absence of the reinforcing effects of alcohol. It is assumed that this stops the reinforcement of the conditioned craving response and extinguishes it. For example, the sight and smell of the client's preferred beverage is presented without allowing drinking to take place. Thus, the conditioned craving response to visual and olfactory cues associated with drinking gradually disappears, or at least is weakened, and the likelihood of relapse when the client encounters such cues in the natural environment decreases.

Cue exposure treatment is related to a very large body of theory and research on classical conditioning in animals and human beings, an extensive literature on its use in other disorders, and a growing body of experimental and clinical research on alcohol and drug dependence *(193)*. This is a reason for its exciting potential as an advance in treatment effectiveness. Nevertheless, many important theoretical and practical issues remain to be resolved. For example, when cue exposure works, how it works is not clear. One point of view maintains that this has little to do with the extinction of conditioned responses and much more to do with an increase in "self-efficacy" as a result of experiences of mastery over alcohol craving *(194)*. Certainly, most authorities accept that cognitive processes – expectations and beliefs – make a very important contribution to the cue exposure process, and that treatment procedures should take account of them *(193)*.

Cue exposure can be directed at both drinking goals: abstinence and moderation. In the former case, cue exposure is intended to decrease the probability of the initiation of drinking in response to internal and external cues formerly associated with drinking *(11,195)*. In the case of the moderation goal, a priming dose of alcohol is used to stimulate craving, which is then extinguished by preventing further drinking from taking place, so that the desire to continue drinking after low amounts is presumably weakened *(196)*. The client may perceive this simply as practice in limiting drinking to low levels. For both goals, cue exposure can be viewed as a kind of inoculation against excessive drinking.

A favoured use of cue exposure at present is to combine it with coping skills training; Monti et al. *(11)* have described such a combined programme. An interesting development is the use of mood induction (including hypnosis) to evoke and extinguish craving among clients especially prone to seek intoxication in response to various mood states, but this procedure is still in the experimental stage. At the very least, the client can be taught to use various cognitive techniques to cope with craving and the urge to drink *(197)*. In addition, exposure to alcohol-related stimuli can be used during treatment to assess the degrees of craving the client is likely to experience in real situations, and to demonstrate the temptation that he or she is likely to experience after treatment. This is an attempt to counteract the overconfidence that so many clients show.

Clinical Research

Early reports on cue exposure were largely confined to case studies, either with *(198)* or without *(195)* the use of a priming dose of alcohol. These reports were highly encouraging, but proper clinical trials of this treatment have been set up only in the last few years.

Monti et al. *(199)* compared cue exposure integrated with coping skills training with standard inpatient treatment, and found a better drinking outcome among clients receiving cue exposure during the second three months after treatment. Similarly, Drummond & Glautier *(200)* compared cue exposure with relaxation and found more favourable outcome for cue exposure, in terms of length of time to relapse to heavy drinking and of total alcohol consumption at follow-up six months after treatment. Following the description by Heather et al. *(196)* of moderation-oriented cue exposure among clients with low-to-medium alcohol dependence, a clinical trial is evaluating the effectiveness of this method in comparison with conventional moderation training (behavioural self-control training). In general, clinical research on cue exposure is proceeding in various parts of the world and its results are awaited with great interest.

POTENTIAL OF COGNITIVE–BEHAVIOURAL APPROACHES

This chapter has presented evidence suggesting that, among existing forms of treatment for alcohol problems, cognitive–behavioural approaches include the methods that are most strongly supported by adequately designed research. This is reason enough to be optimistic about their potential to improve the overall success rates of treatment for all kinds of problem drinkers.

Another reason for cautious optimism, however, is the fact that cognitive–behavioural approaches arise from and are intimately bound up with a much wider body of behavioural theory and research, one that ensures continuous feedback on their effectiveness and a continuing effort to improve the understanding of treatment processes and of optimal applications. For this reason, cognitive–behavioural methods have been more intensively evaluated than any other category of treatment for alcohol problems. Thus, for the first time in its history, treatment in this field has been placed squarely in the realm of scientific exploration and advancement. This ensures that cognitive–behavioural approaches will not follow the example of previous treatments in the field by continuing to be widely applied without either theoretical justification or sound evidence of effectiveness. Cognitive–behavioural treatments may not be the last word on effective methods in this area, but they have a built-in mechanism – scientific evaluation – to ensure their own improvement or possible replacement by something better.

11

Relapse Prevention and Aftercare

In common with addictive behaviour of all kinds, alcohol dependence is a condition involving a high risk of relapse. Evidence suggests that more than two thirds of clients of treatment programmes for alcohol problems relapse within six months after treatment *(8)*; as time after treatment goes by, fewer and fewer people are able to retain its benefits. The main task in treatment is not to help the client initially to stop or reduce drinking, which is relatively easy, but to ensure the continuation of that change in behaviour. This is why treatment programmes that report their success rates directly after treatment has ended give a most misleading picture of their effectiveness.

During the late 1970s and early 1980s, this broad insight formed the basis for an upsurge in theory and research on the determinants of relapse, and in the development of intervention programmes to help clients resist relapse. Most of this work was based on social learning theory *(201)*. Chief among students of relapse at this time were G. Alan Marlatt and his colleagues, and the greater part of this chapter is devoted to their work.

In terms of the stages of change model, Chapter 8 of this book addressed the precontemplation and contemplation stages, in which the task of intervention is primarily to motivate a person to change drinking behaviour. Chapters 9 and 10 discussed the action stage and the effort to initiate desirable changes in drinking. This chapter is located in the maintenance stage and focuses on the challenge of maintaining the gains made during treatment and preventing relapse. It is assumed that factors central to the maintenance of behaviour change may be quite different from the determinants of initial change.

The length of this chapter, in comparison with that of the previous two chapters, may give the impression that relapse prevention is relatively unimportant. If so, this would be most unfortunate. No treatment service aspiring to effectiveness can afford to ignore this issue.

RELAPSE PREVENTION

A crucial aspect of the new perspective on relapse, introduced by Marlatt & Gordon *(8)*, is how both the therapist and client conceptualize and implicitly define it. In the disease view, a return to drinking is a recurrence of symptoms and evidence of a continuing disease process; it amounts, by definition, to an end-state and a failure of treatment. This encourages a black-and-white perspective on treatment outcome in which the client either does not drink and is cured or does drink and has relapsed.

This traditional, dichotomous view of relapse has a number of unhelpful consequences. For example, to the extent that the client assimilates this perspective during treatment, any return to drinking of whatever degree will lead to the expectation of a full-blown relapse to the level of heavy drinking that existed before treatment began. Since any violation of the rule of abstinence is viewed as total failure, the mechanism of the self-fulfilling prophecy makes such a relapse to pre-treatment drinking likely to occur. Moreover, the cause of this relapse is attributed to mysterious biological factors. The client assumes there is nothing he or she can do about it and feels like the helpless victim of the underlying disease process.

In contrast to this highly pessimistic view of relapse, Marlatt & Gordon *(8)* have described an alternative perspective in which an episode of drinking after treatment is seen as a single act of transgression or a slip: a lapse rather than a relapse. Rather than regarding a full relapse as inevitable and out of his or her control, the client learns that the consequences of the slip are matters that are intimately linked with his or her reactions to it. Furthermore, the client is encouraged to view the event as a learning experience from which valuable lessons can be drawn for the avoidance of future slips.

The Relapse Model

A complete account of the Marlatt & Gordon *(8)* social learning model of relapse is beyond the scope of this book and the interested reader is referred to the original source. A useful description can also be found in Annis & Davis *(202)*. Only a few of the main features of the model are briefly covered here.

Fig. 5 shows the model in diagram form. The first concept of importance is the high-risk situation: one in which the client has a high probability of relapse. Cummings et al. *(203)* identified a range of possible high-risk situations applying to a number of types of addictive behaviour, and interviewed problem drinkers about the frequency with which these situations had been associated with relapse in the past. The three most common situations were: negative emotional states (such as frustration, anger, anxiety, depression or boredom), conflicts with other people and social pressure to drink (either direct, in the form of verbal persuasion, or indirect, in the sense of simply observing others drinking).

If the client can cope with the high-risk situation, he or she experiences a sense of mastery and control over that situation, and an increase in self-efficacy for dealing with subsequent situations of the same kind; the probability of relapse decreases. Problems arise when the client lacks an adequate coping response. In these circumstances, he or she is liable to experience a decrease in self-efficacy and a feeling of helplessness to deal with the situation. If, moreover, he or she expects a positive outcome from the use of alcohol (has learned to expect that drinking will provide an immediate and temporary way of coping), the likelihood of a return to drinking greatly increases. Whether or not this initial lapse leads to further drinking depends, as indicated above, on how the client perceives the lapse. Specifically, the abstinence violation effect (or the rule violation effect in the case of a moderation goal) propels the client towards a full relapse. The strength of this effect depends on a number of factors, including the degree of prior commitment to abstinence and the duration of the abstinence period. The abstinence violation effect is said to consist of

Fig. 5. The social learning model of relapse to substance use

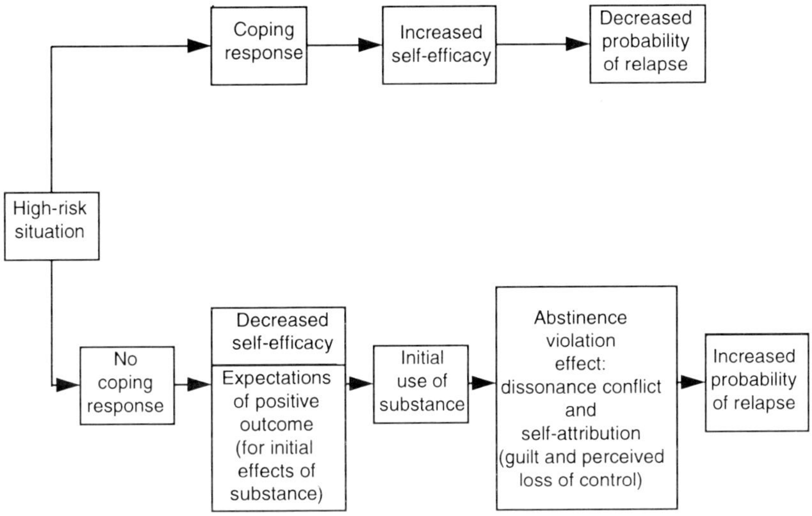

Source: Marlatt & Gordon *(8)*.

two components: cognitive dissonance (feelings of guilt and conflict about the discrepancy between values and behaviour) and a personal attribution effect (blaming factors in the self as the cause of the relapse).

The client's encounter with a high-risk situation is largely considered to be accidental, or at least unavoidable in view of the client's behaviour pattern. The situation can also arise, however, by some sort of subconscious process in which the individual makes a series of decisions that have the effect of placing him or her in a high-risk situation. These are known as seemingly irrelevant decisions; they are targets for modification in a relapse prevention programme.

The Marlatt & Gordon coping model of relapse *(8)* has been criticized. For example, Saunders & Allsop *(204)* have maintained that relapses often have a more consciously planned quality than is evident in the model, and are more a question of commitment and resolution than a matter of coping skills. Heather & Stallard *(205)* have argued that the role of conditioned craving in response to alcohol-related cues is neglected in the model. In later commentary

Marlatt *(206)* has given a greater role in the model to conditioned craving and increased the use of cue exposure techniques. Despite these criticisms, the Marlatt & Gordon model has considerable explanatory value and has rightly been highly influential on treatment.

Assessment and Intervention Procedures

Marlatt & Gordon *(8)* have described assessment and intervention procedures to be used in conjunction with a relapse prevention programme. Annis & Davis *(202)* have provided a complete description of their own relapse prevention programme based on similar, cognitive–behavioural principles. Jarvis et al. *(14)* have given a short guide to relapse prevention methods, and McCrady *(207)* has described a relapse prevention programme for use in couples therapy.

Relapse prevention methods can be divided into specific intervention strategies and global self-control strategies. The goal of the specific strategies is to help the client recognize and anticipate high-risk situations, learn alternative ways of coping with these situations and modify cognitive and emotional reactions to them. The first step is to identify the high-risk situations applying to the case; the inventory of drinking situations (see Chapter 3) can be used here. On this basis, a hierarchy of high-risk situations, ranging from the least to the most tempting, can be constructed for each client and used to order progressively more difficult tasks in homework assignments and relapse rehearsal sessions at the clinic.

The client's self-efficacy for dealing with each high-risk situation can be assessed by the situational confidence questionnaire, supplemented by the more behavioural situational competency test (see Chapter 3) if desired. An assessment of the client's existing coping resources should include environmental, behavioural, cognitive and affective areas. In the early stages of treatment, the client can be encouraged simply to avoid high-risk situations, but this is impractical in some cases. In any event, training the client to confront high-risk situations without relapse gives the best results.

The development of skills to cope with high-risk situations involves the training methods discussed in the previous chapter.

Depending on the client's particular coping deficits, these may cover anxiety management, anger management, assertiveness, communication and other social skills, as well as more general problem-solving skills. The whole range of procedures, including instruction, behaviour rehearsal, role play, modelling and evaluative feedback, can be employed. In relapse prevention training, the client learns to be his or her own therapist, since high-risk situations continue to occur after the formal treatment programme has ended. It is hoped that, having successfully practised coping skills in specific high-risk situations, the client can apply them to other tempting situations.

The second set of techniques in the specific relapse prevention strategies focuses on the client's reactions after a slip or temporary return to drinking has taken place, as it does in many cases. The therapist can draw up an explicit therapeutic contract as to the steps to take in this event, and bolster it by giving the client a reminder card with instructions to read and follow. The therapist should work out this contract with the client, but it can include such devices as telephoning the treatment centre or a helpful friend. Cognitive restructuring techniques are aimed at helping the client to counteract the cognitive and affective aspects of the abstinence violation effect, and preventing the lapse from turning into a full-blown relapse.

The global self-control part of the relapse prevention programme encourages a comprehensive change in lifestyle to make relapse less likely. It is thought that one important background reason for relapse is the client's feeling that his or her lifestyle is dominated by a list of duties and obligations, and lacks the opportunity for gratifying experiences. The aim is to develop a lifestyle that restores the balance between the two. In other words, the client is encouraged to find avenues for gratifying experiences that do not involve alcohol intoxication. This may involve taking up so-called positive addictions, such as meditation or physical exercise *(8)*. Such lifestyle changes are thought to be the best defence against the covert motivational processes described as seemingly irrelevant decisions.

Finally, the client should receive help to control the occasional urges and cravings for alcohol that inevitably arise in spite of carefully planned avoidance and coping strategies. In one useful method known as urge surfing, the client is taught to ride out the peak intensities of the craving experience in the same manner as a surfer deals with big waves at sea.

The main principle underlying all these techniques is that the client's interests are best served by anticipating and fully discussing the possibilities for relapse with the therapist during the active treatment phase, to prepare for the temptation that will undoubtedly arise. Traditional treatment programmes avoided the discussion of relapse because it was believed somehow to give the client permission to relapse. The philosophy of relapse prevention treatment is based on the entirely different assumption that anticipating and preparing for high-risk situations, in the same way that a fire-drill anticipates and prepares for a fire, is the best way to avoid their destructive consequences.

Effectiveness

The evidence on the effectiveness of elements of the broad spectrum approach and various skills training methods, reviewed in the previous chapter, can be considered to support the relapse prevention approach. This is because these methods are intended to teach the skills and cognitions identified as new coping behaviour in the relapse prevention model. Especially relevant is the study by Chaney et al. *(51)*, who based their training method on the types of relapse situation identified by Cummings et al. *(203)*. In addition, good evidence supports the role in relapse of some of the central concepts of the model, such as self-efficacy *(202)*.

Evaluations of relapse prevention programmes in the form of a self-contained package have produced somewhat less encouraging results. Annis and her colleagues *(202)* compared a group of clients who had been randomly allocated to relapse prevention training following a three-week inpatient programme with a group that received traditional counselling. Among clients who had differentiated profiles on the inventory of drinking situations, in which risks of drinking were greater in some situations than in others, those who received relapse prevention showed a substantially lower consumption at follow-up after six months. Among the clients showing a generalized profile, in which drinking risk was similar for all high-risk situations, there was no difference between the two groups. This suggests that a relapse prevention programme is effective when procedures can be focused on specific situations and skills, but not when the risk of relapse is more diffuse. In the latter case, the existing type of relapse prevention programme may require modification. Other research of variable quality has failed to find a favourable effect from relapse prevention training *(3)* and work in this area continues. The next section deals with the effectiveness of relapse prevention training given after the end of formal treatment.

AFTERCARE

Relapse prevention has been described as occurring during formal treatment, either as a principle of intervention influencing the entire programme or as a topic covered towards the end. The goal is to assist the client to prepare for the temptations that will arise after treatment in the hope of maintaining treatment gains. This section considers ways of maintaining these gains in aftercare programmes scheduled at various intervals after the active treatment phase has concluded. The evidence suggests that aftercare arrangements can make a crucial contribution to the client's recovery. Indeed, some would argue that good aftercare is the most important ingredient of a successful treatment service *(208)*. Certainly, there is good evidence to suggest that post-treatment factors – chiefly those to do with the home environment – have a greater effect on outcome than the client's pre-treatment characteristics *(209)*.

One frequently used form of aftercare is referral to AA or to other self-help groups. The next chapter considers the effectiveness of AA. Here one may merely note that AA is acceptable to only a proportion of problem drinkers; other kinds of aftercare are necessary.

Aftercare has usually followed inpatient treatment but can in principle be scheduled to follow treatment in any setting. As inpatient services are likely to be reduced in future, an aftercare phase following formal discharge from an outpatient programme will become increasingly common.

It is no use relying on some kind of informal aftercare arrangement in which the client is left to get in touch with the clinic for a brief chat at some unspecified time in the future. Even scheduling an appointment is not sufficient unless special efforts are made to ensure that the client keeps the appointment. Aftercare should not be seen as some kind of optional extra but as an essential component of the treatment service, and pains should be taken to make the client understand this. Thus, a structured and carefully planned aftercare programme is needed, with specific procedures to encourage attendance.

Purposes

In addition to the general aim of maintaining treatment gains, structured aftercare can have the following purposes:

1. to enable the early detection of a relapse and attempts to limit its negative consequences;
2. to help to prevent a lapse from turning into a full relapse;
3. to provide an opportunity to evaluate the usefulness of the new skills and behaviour that the client has practised, including life-style changes, and to discuss any problems that may have arisen;
4. to provide specific booster sessions for skills and behavioural changes that need strengthening; and
5. to monitor and record progress and to reinforce the client's success.

Aftercare can be run on either an individual or a group basis. The former obviously offers more opportunity to consider the client's unique problems in adjustment and any specific coping deficits that remain. On the other hand, groups can provide a useful support network and the chance to learn from other people's mistakes. In addition, attention should be paid to mundane but crucial practical matters, such as housing problems and access to welfare entitlements. The services of a social worker may be needed for this.

As to the timing of aftercare appointments, three, six and twelve months after treatment is standard. Some clients, however, may need to be seen before three months or more frequently. Although aftercare programmes should be highly structured, they should also be flexible to accommodate individual needs and circumstances.

Jarvis et al. *(14)* have briefly described aftercare principles and procedures. O'Farrell *(210)* has described a complete relapse prevention programme for couples to follow behavioural marital therapy, with good evidence of effectiveness.

Encouraging Attendance

As suggested above, an aftercare programme, no matter how skilfully designed, is ineffective if clients ignore it. Unfortunately, rates of attrition commonly found at, for example, three months after treatment are roughly 50%. Special procedures to decrease attrition are clearly needed.

Some very simple devices can be helpful. The client can be provided with a calendar indicating appointment times; he or she can be sent a reminder letter or telephoned a week before the next appointment. If the client misses an appointment for any reason, another one should be scheduled as soon as possible and, when the client does arrive, the reasons for the missed appointment should be carefully discussed. Probably most important, the therapist should prepare the client for aftercare before the active treatment phase has ended, by clearly explaining its purposes and its vital importance in the recovery process.

In a very useful development, Ossip-Klein & Rychtarik *(211)* have described the use of behavioural contracts between the problem drinkers and family members to improve participation in aftercare. Controlled research has shown this method to be effective in improving attendance rates.

In addition to arranging aftercare appointments, the therapist should encourage the client to initiate contact with the treatment service whenever he or she feels the need for help. The client must see the service as an open, welcoming organization that will not criticize or punish lapses.

Effectiveness

Although the amount of research on aftercare is not large, the evidence in its favour is impressive. Ahles et al. *(212)* compared a group of male problem drinkers given aftercare, arranged by the behavioural contracting method referred to above, with a control group given aftercare scheduled session by session. At follow-up after one year, the rate of abstinence was 40% in the experimental group and 11% in the control group.

In an evaluation of their couples relapse prevention programme, O'Farrell et al. *(213)* showed that the addition of the programme to behavioural marital therapy significantly improved drinking and marital outcomes among male problem drinkers and their spouses. Ito & Donovan *(208)* carefully reviewed the available evidence on the effects of aftercare and concluded that it was an important and effective type of intervention for alcohol problems.

12

Alcoholics Anonymous and Other Self-help Groups

ALCOHOLICS ANONYMOUS

No discussion of treatment for alcohol problems would be complete without consideration of the Fellowship of Alcoholics Anonymous (AA), although in many ways it could be more accurately described as a way of life than a form of treatment. In the United States following the lifting of national prohibition of alcohol during the 1930s, political and scientific interest in alcohol problems was almost zero and other countries showed the same lack of interest. A small group of men and women, who had experienced severe problems with drinking, filled the breach and provided help for the increasing number of people who found they could not control their drinking. AA is usually called a self-help group, but the name mutual aid group would be more accurate.

Since the 1930s, AA has expanded at a remarkable rate. By the end of the 1980s, it had spread to all continents of the globe and reported a total membership of 1.5 million people *(214)*. Despite this wide diffusion, AA remains strongest in the developed and relatively wealthy countries of the world, although some progress has recently been observed in newly industrialized nations. Aside from the dramatic increase in its membership, AA has been highly successful in promoting its image of alcoholism to the general public and relevant professional groups, to the point at which many people's understanding of alcohol problems has become synonymous with AA views and where it is regarded as the best, if not the only, solution to a drinking problem. In addition, AA has become well integrated with formal treatment services. Some medical specialists in the field still regard AA as the most appropriate form of continuing care for all their clients, and AA principles continue to dominate the national treatment scene in the United States. The penetration of the treatment world by AA affiliates is extensive in some countries, particularly in the United States.

From the point of view of treatment policy, the great attraction of AA is that it is entirely self-financing and therefore places no burden whatever on the national exchequer. From the problem drinker's point of view, it is highly accessible and offers help on a continuous, 24-hour basis. Despite the reservations about aspects of AA in this chapter, it has unquestionably saved the lives of huge numbers of people all over the world and is an extremely valuable resource in any country's battle against alcohol-related harm.

Characteristics

The characteristics of AA are too well known to bear much repetition here. Members of AA believe that they suffer from a disease that is present before they ever come into contact with alcohol and that results in a permanent inability to control drinking. The disease of alcoholism afflicts only a small minority of drinkers; it cannot be cured but only arrested by total and lifelong abstinence. Further drinking leads invariably to progressive deterioration, insanity or death.

The code of AA principles and practice *(111)* finds expression in 12 steps, supported by 12 traditions; the references to "a higher power" in this code reveal the strong spiritual element in AA teaching. A crucial feature of the AA recovery programme is the practice known as "twelfth stepping", in which an established member takes responsibility for helping and advising a new recruit. This is regarded as essential to the recovery of both. This activity is supported by regular meetings at which the recovering alcoholics tell their personal stories, much in the manner of an evangelical prayer meeting. The AA recruit is urged to attend these meetings almost every night at first and then on a regular basis for the rest of his or her life.

The spiritual teaching of AA, in an experience akin to religious conversion, seems likely to be responsible for its success in many cases. The social organization of AA, which provides strong support for a new life without alcohol and indeed an entirely new self-concept and social identity, however, is probably also crucial. As implied above, no formal treatment service can match AA in the continuity of support it offers to its new adherents. Robinson *(215)* and McCrady & Irvine *(216)* provide further description of and comment on AA.

Effectiveness

Unfortunately, conducting research on the effectiveness of AA has proved extremely difficult, mainly because of the anonymity that it properly insists on and the problems in forming randomized control groups. AA itself has no doubt of its effectiveness, with success rates of over 75% having been put forward. Rates such as this may apply to the small group of total converts who persevere with regular attendance over a number of years, but they must be regarded with considerable scepticism as a general statement of outcome among all those who attend or are referred to AA.

Summaries of controlled research on AA *(5,216)* show that only two studies *(176,217)* have succeeded in randomly assigning problem drinkers to AA or to other forms of intervention. Neither showed any advantage for AA and one *(176)* showed a poorer retention rate for subjects assigned to AA. Both these studies use court-referred problem drinkers, however, who had been forced to attend for treatment. Such clients have poor prospects of success in any form of treatment. Moreover, it could be argued that involuntary referral to a voluntary organization such as AA limits the chances of effectiveness.

As anticipated in the Introduction, it cannot be concluded that research has shown AA to be ineffective for the general run of problem drinking clients. All that can be said is that research does not support its effectiveness. McCrady & Miller *(218)* make suggestions for further research on AA.

Matching Clients

Although the only requirement for membership of AA is a desire to stop drinking, there are good reasons to believe it is helpful to particular kinds of individual. Of all those who initially attend AA or are referred to it by professional workers, only a relatively small proportion are likely to attend regularly *(219)*, the rest either attending on a spasmodic basis or dropping out completely. Those who do attend regularly, however, are likely to have a good outcome. What are the characteristics of these individuals?

Ogborne & Glaser *(220)* have reviewed the literature on the characteristics of successful affiliates. The evidence suggests, first, that AA is suited to people of a more authoritarian personality, who tend to see the world in black-and-white terms and are intolerant of ambiguity. Other work suggests that successful affiliates have a stronger need for affiliation than most people and, as might be expected, are overtly religious in personal orientation or at least have strong spiritual concerns. Although AA groups differ widely between countries and cultures, there is also evidence that they appeal more to problem drinkers who are white, socially stable and middle-class than to those in lower classes or from other ethnic backgrounds. More recently, Emrick *(219)* had much more difficulty finding clear differences between problem drinkers who had affiliated with AA and those who had not.

The results of Project MATCH (see page 40) will much improve the understanding of the best way to match clients with AA. Although the Project is concerned with the effectiveness of an outpatient twelve-step programme and not with AA itself, the results will be of considerable relevance.

Meanwhile, one can safely conclude that, while certain types of problem drinker may be best suited to AA, others – probably the majority of problem drinkers – do not find it helpful or acceptable. In secular societies, many are put off by the spiritual aspects of AA teaching and others have difficulty in revealing the details of their personal lives in public. There are probably many reasons why AA is not appropriate for all problem drinkers, in the same way that no specific formal treatment approach is suitable for all clients. This again argues the need for a range of alternative treatment approaches to be made available.

Drawbacks of the Alcoholism Image

Although the kind of help AA offers has several advantages, its image of alcoholism can be seen as a hindrance to progress, especially in early intervention and secondary prevention. In terms of drinking history and type of alcohol problem, regular AA attenders usually have more serious problems than average, typically in the mould of the familiar picture of severe physical dependence with dramatic withdrawal symptoms, extremely high tolerance, classic amnesic episodes and complete loss of control over consumption. In AA parlance, drinkers have to have reached rock-bottom and to have experienced a great deal of suffering and harm to themselves and their families before they will be prepared to abjure alcohol for life.

Given this image of alcohol problems, AA is most unlikely to be acceptable to people whose problems are less serious or of more recent origin (see Chapter 7). The difficulty is that this portrayal of alcoholism (mainly as a consequence of media publicity) is so widely accepted that a member of the general public is likely to think this is the only kind of alcohol problem that exists, anything less dramatic and serious being of little consequence. This view encourages problem drinkers in the early stages to ignore incipient signs of harm, to deny that they have a problem or, if they recognize a problem, to deny that they need help. Thus, efforts to reach drinkers earlier in the course of their problems or to introduce a public health understanding of the wider damage caused by alcohol in society are impeded.

The lessons from this analysis are obvious. Alcohol specialists must take pains to educate the general public and professional groups, especially the general medical practitioners who it is hoped will deliver brief interventions (see Chapter 7), that this portrayal of alcohol problems is deeply misleading. This does not suggest that the heroic work done by AA should be denigrated, but that AA views of the issue of alcohol in society and its propagation of these views have unhelpful effects.

OTHER SELF-HELP GROUPS

Two organizations provide help for families of problem drinkers: Alanon for spouses and Alateen for teenage children. Although these have not undergone any formal evaluation, they are widely used and there is little doubt that they provide valuable support.

Other types of self-help group may arise in different countries and are responsive to the cultural conditions from which they spring. Some may be aimed at moderate drinking rather than abstinence. Davies *(221)* has described one such group in Finland, called the Polar Bears. Ruzek *(222)* has reported on an organization in the United Kingdom called Drinkwatchers.

Rational Recovery

Velten *(223)* has described and commented on an interesting alternative to AA, known as rational recovery. Rational recovery is mainly confined to the United States, where groups are said to meet in about 500 cities and towns, but is beginning to attract attention in other parts of the world. Rational recovery is essentially a self-help version of rational emotive behaviour therapy *(170)* and is specifically intended for those who are not attracted to AA. It challenges the AA assumptions about a permanent disease status and the necessity for continuing attendance at meetings.

The promise of rational recovery is that it may be able to retain some of the advantages of the AA type of organization – the group cohesion, the social support for a new lifestyle, the constant availability of help and the high cost–effectiveness – while abandoning the spiritual side that deters many problem drinkers from AA and the underlying disease theory that has proved so unhelpful. No published data are yet available on the effectiveness of rational recovery, but it is to be hoped that these will be forthcoming. Velten *(223)* has also described another secular self-help organization in the United States, Women for Sobriety.

Twelve-step Programmes

In addition to its phenomenal success, AA has spawned a large number of self-help groups and treatment programmes in the United States for nearly every conceivable kind of problem in living. This has brought about a huge addictions treatment industry *(224)*. Confining attention here to alcohol problems, one may note the proliferation of the Adult Children of Alcoholics (ACOA) and co-dependency movements.

ACOA is founded on evidence that the children of people with severe alcohol problems have a higher risk of such problems in later life and sometimes have psychological problems without harmful use of alcohol. ACOA goes far beyond this evidence, however, to promote an all-embracing social movement in which all who might consider that one of their parents are or were an alcoholic are invited to immerse themselves in regular group meetings. The co-dependency movement extended this idea to all family members of the problem drinker, and added the notion that the actions of those who try to cope with the problem drinker's behaviour can be seen as secret attempts to encourage or enable heavy drinking for unconscious reasons of their own. As Velten *(223)* points out, the so-called disease of co-dependency includes essentially all aspects of human unhappiness; hence its potentially huge market for new customers.

Velten *(223)* has severely criticized the social effects of both these mass movements. Not only is there no evidence that they are effective in helping relatives or friends of problem drinkers, their far-fetched claims have no scientific basis whatever. Indeed, these movements appear to have been designed to be impervious to evidence of any kind.

The Minnesota Model

In the United States another off-shoot of AA has been the growth of private, profit-making treatment for alcohol problems based on twelve-step principles. The most commonly encountered are known as Minnesota model (or Hazelden-type) programmes. For some time, the companies in question have been attempting to promote their products overseas, in parts of Europe as well as elsewhere.

Cook *(225)* has described the philosophy and programme of the Minnesota model. The philosophy is based on the assumption that the client has an incurable biological and personality disease, characterized by denial. Thus, the programme usually takes the form of lengthy inpatient treatment involving intensive group therapy and harsh confrontation of the problem drinker's alleged denial.

As shown in Chapter 8, there is no evidence that confrontation is effective in the treatment of alcohol problems, and more than a suggestion that it is counterproductive. Moreover, Chapter 7 showed that inpatient programmes represent an extremely cost-ineffective response to alcohol problems; for the problem drinkers who can afford to attend Minnesota model programmes and who often have the social stability to possess a good prognosis, they are likely to be even less cost-effective than for the normal run of problem drinkers. While problem drinkers and their families obviously have the right to spend their money as they think fit, the expenditure of public funds on treatment by the Minnesota model has no rational justification.

One controlled trial of the impact of the Minnesota model has been reported in the literature. Keso & Salaspuro *(226)* compared treatment at a Hazelden-type institute with traditional treatment that consisted of inpatient psychiatric care and social work. They found that the Hazelden-type treatment produced higher abstinence rates at a follow-up after one year. In addition, the twelve-step programme was able to retain substantially more clients in treatment.

One should note, however, that this was a comparison of two forms of inpatient treatment. It would perhaps have been more instructive to have compared the Hazelden-type programme with an outpatient form of treatment, when considerations of cost–effectiveness would be highly relevant. Once again, the results of Project MATCH may tell a great deal about the effects of twelve-step programmes compared with cognitive–behavioural therapy, and how these two quite different forms of treatment can be matched to client characteristics.

13

Costs, Benefits and Effectiveness

People who provide treatment for alcohol problems need little persuading that the importance of economic issues related to treatment is likely to continue to increase. They recognize that government agencies and other sources of funding for treatment programmes will increasingly expect evidence of not only their effectiveness, but also their cost–effectiveness in comparison with other types of treatment for alcohol problems and with other forms of health care.

It is often pointed out that the increasing expense of medical technology and the greater longevity of the population are diminishing the total availability of health care resources. Even in the comparatively rich countries of the world, resources are unlikely to be sufficient to meet all society's demands for health care, and under governments of any political complexion even in times of economic boom. Treatment for alcohol problems must compete with other areas of health care for limited resources.

Some treatment providers are nevertheless anxious about the consequences of applying economic principles to treatment. It is feared that a tendency towards cheaper treatments would inevitably mean second-rate services and, as a consequence, worse-off clients. Even these doubters, however, could surely raise no rational opposition to the principle of using the least expensive of equally effective forms of treatment. Fig. 6 shows three types of relationship between the effectiveness of treatment and costs. A relationship of type A, in which more expensive treatments are less effective, poses no problem in deciding which to prefer. The conclusion is equally straightforward for relationships of type C: if two treatments show no difference in effectiveness, the cheaper should obviously be preferred.

Fig. 6. Three types of relationship between the effectiveness and costs of treatment

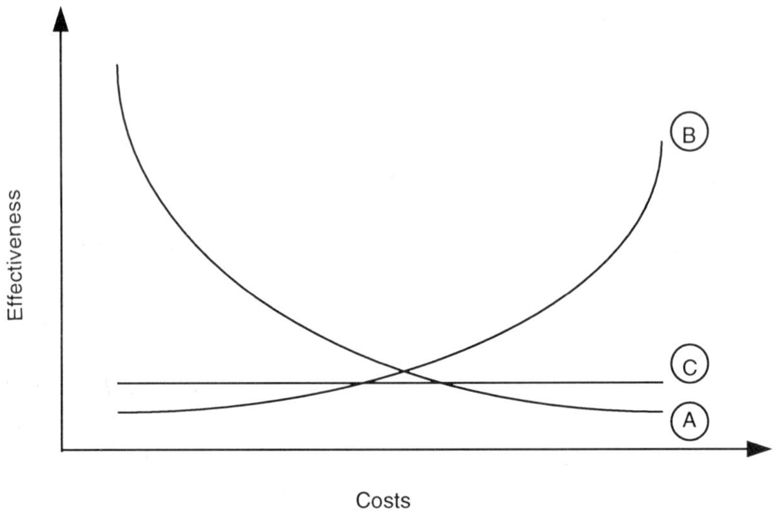

Source: Holder et al. *(4)*.

Problems only arise in the case of a relationship of type B, in which the more effective treatments are also more expensive. There may be little justification for preferring a cheaper treatment if it is less cost-effective than a more expensive one (if the cost per successful outcome were greater). This would imply that the more expensive treatment is much more effective. What happens, however, if the cheaper treatment is somewhat less effective but more cost-effective than the expensive treatment, a situation which is likely to arise? Should one prefer a treatment that may produce less overall benefit for clients who receive it but may, because of its lower costs, be made available to more problem drinkers? This is a difficult ethical dilemma.

The economist's answer to this question would probably be that the cheaper and more cost-effective alternative should be preferred.

This is because of economists' insistence that the costs of a treatment must include its opportunity costs. This concept is based on the principle that every use of resources involves the loss of other opportunities for their use. In other words, resources for treating alcohol problems cannot be considered in isolation but must be placed in a wider context of all health care resources; savings made by using a more cost-effective treatment for alcohol problems are released for other health care purposes. The task of economic evaluation is to try to ensure that the benefits of implementing a treatment programme exceed its opportunity costs.

Incidentally, the conclusion from the analysis by Holder et al. *(4)* is that treatment for alcohol problems shows a relationship between cost and effectiveness similar to type A: the cheaper treatments are actually the more effective. Holder et al. have been criticized for not comparing like with like – in particular, for not recognizing that brief interventions, which appear to be not only cheaper but also more effective than more intensive interventions, were carried out with problem drinkers who had less serious problems and therefore better prognoses than those involved in the studies of more intensive treatments *(227)*. To generalize widely but conservatively from the evidence, however, one can claim that the relationship is of type C; that is, there is no good evidence that effectiveness increases with expense.

TYPES OF ECONOMIC EVALUATION

The several types of economic evaluation flow from the central principle of opportunity costs. For the purposes of this chapter, it is sufficient to distinguish between the two main forms, cost–benefit analysis and cost–effectiveness analysis.

Cost–benefit analysis is used to determine the absolute efficiency of a particular type or goal of health care, and whether a form of treatment or specific treatment programme can demonstrate economic efficiency in itself. It does this by converting all costs and benefits associated with treatment into a common base of measurement, almost always money. For present purposes, cost–benefit analysis would be most often used to answer the question of whether treatment for alcohol problems is worth doing at all: whether it is an efficient use of society's resources compared with doing nothing. Less radically, cost–benefit analysis addresses the question of whether more or less of society's resources should be allocated to the treatment of alcohol problems.

Cost–effectiveness analysis deals with relative efficiency and compares two or more methods of arriving at the same goals. It assumes that a certain goal – say, the reduction of alcohol-related problems by treatment – has been agreed to be worth while, and seeks to determine the most economically efficient way of pursuing this goal.

COST-OFFSETS OF TREATMENT FOR ALCOHOL PROBLEMS

The harmful use of alcohol and alcohol dependence produce considerable costs to society. In particular, alcohol problems and dependence are associated with high medical costs from related organic damage, accidents and injuries. Moreover, problem drinkers and their families consume health care resources at a higher rate than those with no alcohol problem *(228)*. Does the treatment of alcohol problems reduce these costs? Does it pay for itself in later health care savings? Can it produce a net benefit for the health care system? In short, does treatment for alcohol problems produce cost-offsets? Cost–benefit analysis can answer these questions, and some relevant research has been carried out in the United States.

As part of a wider review, Jones & Vischi *(229)* looked at 12 studies that had considered the impact of treatment on the utilization of medical care. They concluded that all these studies demonstrated a reduction in care utilization, either by direct measures such as inpatient days and outpatient visits or by more indirect measures such as sick days and sickness benefits. They noted nearly a 70% reduction in the number of days spent in hospital, a 40% reduction in outpatient visits, a 27–48% reduction in inpatient and outpatient costs and a 40% median total reduction in medical care utilization across studies.

Using a more sophisticated methodology, Saxe et al. *(230)* re-examined four of the studies previously reviewed by Jones & Vischi, along with two newer studies. They cautiously concluded that some evidence supported the hypothesis that treatment was cost-beneficial and that the benefits of treatment exceeded the costs of providing it. They pointed out that many treatment services available in the United States – mainly inpatient, medically based treatment – were clearly cost-ineffective, there being less expensive ways of reaching the same outcomes.

Holder *(231)* reviewed research published since the analysis of Jones & Vischi *(229)* and claimed these studies had fewer methodological limitations than those in the older literature. Holder concluded that, taken as a group, the studies reviewed confirmed the potential of the treatment of alcohol problems to contribute to sustained reductions in total health care utilization and costs. Reductions in post-treatment costs were found to continue into the fourth and fifth years after the start of treatment.

The interpretation of this line of evidence is not without its difficulties, and the Institute of Medicine *(3)* has thoroughly reviewed the area. One problem is the lack of evidence for cost-offsets among economically and socially disadvantaged groups using publicly funded programmes in the United States. This might be explained by the fact that, compared with the more privileged groups among whom cost-offsets have been shown to exist, the poorer population has more severe medical problems before treatment for alcohol problems begins, and fewer personal and social resources for the maintenance of recovery after treatment *(232)*.

To respect a familiar appeal, more research is clearly needed on cost-offsets. There is an especially urgent need for studies conducted outside the United States. Nevertheless, it is reasonable to conclude from the available evidence that treatment for alcohol problems as a whole produces net gains for the health care system and is therefore a worthwhile and efficient use of financial resources.

TREATMENT AND COST–EFFECTIVENESS

Although cost–effectiveness analysis is increasingly included in outcome studies of treatment, there is as yet little formal research of this nature. What we know about the cost–effectiveness of alcohol problems treatment comes from conventional studies of treatment effectiveness combined with reasonable assumptions about the costs of the modalities being compared.

As noted in Chapter 2, cost–effectiveness conclusions about detoxification are fairly straightforward. Hayashida et al. *(30)* found no differences in effectiveness between inpatient and outpatient detoxification, but estimated their costs as about US $3665–4419 and US $175–388 per patient, respectively. Sparadeo et al. *(27)* reported that the costs per patient for the social setting detoxification unit were roughly 15% of those for inpatient, medicated detoxification. To repeat the conclusions of Chapter 2, a large body of data, reviewed by Greenstreet *(233)*, has shown that both community-based, medicated detoxification and hospital-based, non-medicated detoxification are effective, safe and very much cheaper alternatives to hospital-based, medicated withdrawal. Clear guidelines are available for identifying the exceptional cases in which hospital detoxification is required *(28)*.

The position with regard to treatment proper is far less clear but three issues related to delivery are obviously relevant.

Group Versus Individual Approaches

A common assumption among treatment providers is that, for obvious reasons, group therapy is more cost-effective than individual approaches. This is frequently the main reason for preferring group formats. Sometimes, of course, groups are the only way in which the demand for treatment can be met. There appear, however, to be no empirical studies of cost–effectiveness in this area or even much discussion of the issue.

Two studies *(155,179)* have reported that clients given a group version of a treatment modality had superior outcomes to those receiving an individual version, but the type of treatment involved (social skills training and marital therapy) may have been especially conducive to the group setting. Miller & Taylor *(234)* did not find a difference between group and individual versions of behavioural self-control training, but there does not seem to be any evidence for the superiority of individual treatment. If research eventually confirms that the outcomes of group approaches tend to equal or surpass those of individual approaches, the group version should clearly be preferred on economic grounds in most circumstances. The individual format may be more cost-effective for some types of problem drinker, perhaps more difficult cases, but information is scarce.

AA could be described as a form of group therapy. As seen in Chapter 12, there is little scientific evidence to confirm the effectiveness of AA compared with other treatment methods, but it is highly likely to be effective for certain categories of problem drinker. If this is the case, AA is certain to be a highly cost-effective form of intervention among these people, if only because of the absence of any salaried staff. Again, however, certain kinds of problem drinker seem to be less likely to benefit from AA, and it may be cost-ineffective for them. Similar considerations apply to other forms of mutual aid.

Treatment Setting

Evidence mentioned in Chapter 6 has shown conclusively that inpatient and residential treatment confers no advantage over outpatient and non-residential forms of care for the great majority of problem drinkers, and is therefore much less cost-effective. The costs of day treatment programmes have been estimated at one half *(235)* to one third *(236)* of those of inpatient programmes.

Holder et al. *(4)* have compiled an extensive database for the average cost per client for the unit of care provided by a range of treatment settings and facilities in the United States. Table 6 lists some of these costs for illustrative purposes.

These data distinguish between specific types of setting within the broader categories of inpatient, residential and outpatient treatment. Thus, treatment provided by specialized alcoholism units in hospitals is much more expensive than residential treatment with minimal medical involvement, which is no more expensive than day programmes. Similarly, within the broad category of ambulatory care,

Table 6. Average cost per client of various types of treatment for alcohol problems

Treatment type	Cost per unit (US $ in 1987)
Specialized alcoholism hospital or hospital unit	230 per day
Specialized psychiatric or mental health hospital	330 per day
Residential alcoholism treatment (minimum medical involvement)	70 per day
Hospital-based day programme	70 per day
Outpatient programme	34 per hour/visit
Social model non-residential programme	18 per hour/visit
Alcoholism treatment programmes in community mental health centres with group therapy/counselling	15 per hour
Psychologist (Ph.D.) in private practice therapy/counselling	81 per hour/visit
Psychotherapist (licensed MD in private practice) therapy/counselling	98 per hour/visit

Source: Holder et al. *(4)*.

treatment given by private practitioners, both medical and non-medical, is more than twice as expensive as the average outpatient programme, and group therapy and counselling at community mental health centres is less than half the cost of outpatient care.

The most important general conclusion from Holder et al. *(4)* is that the costs of treatment differ widely with its setting and staffing. Given that very few differences in effectiveness have been found between these forms of treatment, the cheaper should normally be preferred for the majority of problem drinkers. As established in Chapter 6, however, some types of problem drinker may do better in residential settings, such as those with dysfunctional family or work relationships *(237)*, low social stability *(70)* or social disadvantage in general *(238)*. Research is needed to test these hypotheses on matching. In the meantime, it is best to adopt a position based on the burden of proof *(3)*, in which a more expensive treatment setting should be used only when accompanied by a specific justification for making an exception to the rule of cheaper treatment.

Length of Treatment

Length of treatment is perhaps the most important area in the cost–effectiveness analysis of treatment, given the great interest in and enthusiasm for the application of brief interventions. Chapter 7 argues that a crucial distinction should always be made between the use of brief interventions among different populations: those that seek treatment and those that do not. The same distinction is employed in this chapter.

Screening is always necessary with the population seeking treatment, and one must consider the cost–effectiveness of screening as a related but separate issue from that of the interventions themselves. Tolley & Rowland *(239)* compared the cost–effectiveness of using three occupational groups to identify excessive drinkers on general hospital wards – junior medical practitioners, nurses and a specialist worker employed full-time on screening. The specialist worker obtained a higher positive case identification rate but at the greater cost of employing an extra person. Thus, the decision as to whether to create such a position must be a matter of priorities. If this is considered too expensive, it should be noted that nurses were more cost-effective at screening than junior physicians.

As to opportunistic interventions, the main hope, of course, is that early intervention will avert more expensive treatment in the future. From the public health perspective, it is assumed that a reduction in heavy drinking will reduce the general burden from alcohol-related harm in the community. Unfortunately, reasonable though these assumptions may be, there is little evidence at present to support them and such evidence is urgently needed.

The exception here is the work in Sweden by Kristenson et al. *(103)*. It showed that, compared with an experimental group given brief intervention, a control group of middle-aged, male excessive drinkers had a significantly greater increase in mean number of sick days per individual, more total days in hospital and a strikingly greater number of days in hospital for alcohol-related conditions at follow-up after two and four years. At a follow-up after five years, the control group showed twice as many deaths as the experimental group, whether these were probably alcohol-related or not. Although no formal economic evaluation was done, these findings have clear implications for health care savings.

As to the population seeking treatment, Chapter 7 shows some justification for offering a brief intervention to people with a low level of alcohol dependence and to those with more serious problems who prefer it. For those attending treatment for the first time, a stepped care approach can be adopted in which brief interventions are tried first, followed by progressively more intensive treatment in the absence of a favourable response. This stepped care model is described in somewhat more detail in Chapter 15, as part of a comprehensive treatment system. It suffices to say here that the judicious and intelligent use of brief intervention in specialist treatment settings can yield considerable savings.

CONCLUSIONS

In the situation that prevails in all countries – increasingly fierce competition for limited resources from various health care specialties – the economic efficiency of the treatment of alcohol problems is likely to increase in importance.

First, AA and other mutual aid groups are very cost-effective resources for people who are suited to them. Within a specialist service, conducting most treatment in a group format can probably result in substantial savings. Considerable savings can certainly be made by reserving inpatient and residential treatment for only a small minority of clients and treating everyone else on an outpatient or day patient basis. Although suitable prudence should always be exercised, the evidence suggests that a sizeable number of clients can benefit from a relatively brief form of intervention, allowing savings to be made that can be used to provide better services for those who appear to need more intensive treatment.

Although good evidence on the economic justification for brief, opportunistic interventions is awaited, it is reasonable to assume that they result in cost savings for the health care system and in the wider community.

As to the provision of treatment as a whole, the evidence shows that, for the majority of problem drinkers, treatment produces cost-offsets for the health care system. Put another way, not providing treatment for problem drinkers wastes resources.

14

The Role of Coercion in Treatment

Before the implications of the material in this book for treatment delivery can be drawn together in a final chapter, we need to consider a vexed question: the role, if any, of the coercion of problem drinkers into the treatment system.

Various parts of this book have made the distinction between the population that seeks treatment and the one that does not; the latter includes people who are identified in community settings as drinking too much for their own good and are advised to cut down. This has ignored the existence of a third group, which does not seek treatment but is coerced in a variety of ways into receiving it. Some argue that a very large proportion of those receiving treatment for alcohol problems are coerced because they have attended the treatment facility only as a result of pressure from family, employers or medical advisers. Surely, this sort of informal pressure differs from the institutionalized coercion that is the subject of this chapter.

This topic raises complex and difficult ethical, legal and political issues that cannot be resolved here, even assuming that some of them can be satisfactorily resolved at present. Only some very broad conclusions are attempted. It is probably more important, however, that the treatment community and other interested parties openly debate and confront the ethics of coerced treatment, rather than ignoring or brushing aside this issue. This chapter will have succeeded in its main objective if it stimulates such debate.

Involuntary treatment for inebriety was, of course, commonplace during the nineteenth century, and most countries of the world have retained some form of it ever since. More recently, however, the use of coercion has greatly increased in the treatment system for alcohol problems in the United States. Coercion in one form or another largely fuelled the enormous expansion of the alcoholism treatment industry in that country during the 1970s and 1980s *(240,241)*. Although coerced treatment may have increased in other countries of the world, most of the recent literature on the topic has focused on the situation in the United States, which forms the basis for the discussion here. Readers must decide on the relevance of this material for the situation in their own countries.

TYPES OF COERCION

Weisner *(242)* has compiled an extensive review of the use of coercion into treatment in the United States and distinguished four types: civil commitment, diversionary referrals from the criminal justice system, workplace referrals, and early and family intervention programmes. These four types represent a gradient of coercion ranging from more to less explicit and mandatory forms, along which coercion becomes increasingly subtle and unacknowledged.

Civil Commitment

Civil commitment is the most severe and frank type of coercion: the involuntary commitment to treatment of people who are thought to present an imminent danger either to themselves or to others.

Problem drinkers are often committed under the more general rubric of mental illness. This is not the place to discuss the validity of the mental illness concept or the ethical and legal propriety of commitment on these terms. The works of Thomas Szasz make the most forceful objections from a radical libertarian position to both the concept of mental illness itself *(243)* and infringements by the state of individual civil liberties by means of this concept *(244)*. Szasz *(245)* has also commented on the civil liberty issues raised by the concept of addiction.

Weisner *(242)* has noted an increasing tendency in the United States for civil commitments to be carried out under the justification of alcoholism. Such a practice is predicated on the idea that alcoholism is a disease and that the alcoholic is not responsible for his or her actions. This again raises very deep philosophical issues. This idea has been heavily criticized in recent years *(15,246)* and is losing popularity in scientific and treatment circles in many parts of the world. Thus, it can no longer be regarded with complacency as a sound legal and ethical justification for depriving problem drinkers of their civil liberties. Fingarette *(247)* and Conrad & Schneider *(248)* have addressed the legal implications of the disease concept of alcoholism and the legal confusions it has engendered.

The most obvious concern about involuntary commitment and the shift from punishment to treatment on which it is alleged to be based is the fear that frank and acknowledged punishment is in fact replaced by covert punishment, dressed up as treatment but lacking the protection of rights and liberties enshrined in the legal process. This general concern applies to all forms of legally enforced treatment.

Diversions from the Criminal Justice System

A more common form of coerced treatment arises from the practice of diversionary referrals from the courts. These have been used for three main categories of offence: public drunkenness and crimes in which alcohol is directly involved or is alleged to have been a factor.

The move to diversionary schemes for public drunkenness offenders sprang from the good intention of decriminalizing drunkenness. If such schemes involve the complete removal of all legal sanctions and referral to treatment on a purely voluntary basis, this presumably entails few ethical difficulties. In practice, however, diversion typically takes place after conviction by the courts, either before sentencing or at a later point in the process. As such, diversionary treatments are inevitably part of the sanctions imposed on the convicted person, who is normally required satisfactorily to complete treatment in order to avoid further sanctions. Some people accept the advice to enter treatment voluntarily before appearing in court, but they frequently do this to lighten the sentence that will be imposed. Thus, the voluntary nature of the act is questionable.

Given the aim of decriminalizing public drunkenness through diversionary programmes, the success of such programmes both in reducing arrests for drunkenness in the United States and in helping to rehabilitate the offenders is debatable. Finn *(249)* has reported mixed results on this shift from the criminal justice system to the treatment system, and found that the health care system had not, as hoped, improved the physical, emotional or social conditions of offenders.

The second class of offence refers mainly to convictions for drink-driving. Diversionary programmes for drink-drivers have increased at an exponential rate in the United States over the last 25 years, with offenders being mandated by the courts to attend private, fee-paying facilities. The ability of this treatment system to reduce either drink-driving or the general level of alcohol-related problems among these offenders, however, has not been established.

The third category of diversionary schemes involves cases in which the offender shows a history of alcohol problems, or intoxication is held to be in some way responsible for or related to the commission of the crime. Such crimes can range from property offences to domestic violence and other violent offences.

In the last two categories of diversionary schemes, the offender sometimes has a choice of accepting treatment or the sentence of the court. In most cases, however, any rational person would choose the option of treatment, since the court is likely to impose a much more severe and arduous penalty. This looks less like a free choice than a subtle form of coercion. In another example of subtle coercion, the court requires an offender to accept disulfiram. The taking of this drug is apparently voluntary, but non-compliance leads to referral back to the court for alternative sentencing.

In the United States, this kind of sentencing policy has even involved AA. The courts frequently mandate offenders to go to AA and demand proof of attendance at meetings. Given the purely voluntary, self-help origins of the organization and the insistence that the main qualification for membership is a sincere desire to stop drinking, such a policy might be thought antithetical to the AA ethos. It is subject to intense debate within AA.

Workplace Referrals

In addition to drink-drivers, workplace referrals are the other main source of clients for the alcohol treatment industry in the United States. The facilities involved here include employee assistance programmes run by or for large companies and by trade unions, and those for members of particular professions.

The coercive element here is the implication, or sometimes the explicit policy, that the employee must accept treatment as an alternative to dismissal or demotion. The term constructive confrontation *(250)* has come to be applied to this situation but, whether or not it is considered ethically justified, it is clearly another form of coercion. The justification from the employee's perspective is that treatment is preferable to job loss, and from the employer's perspective that retention of the worker's skills and expertise following successful treatment is in the organization's best interests. Excessive drinking by employees is certainly responsible for a considerable loss of productivity in industry and business *(85)*.

The grounds on which workplace referrals are made is an important concern. If these are purely to do with job performance, it can be argued that the employer has a right to insist on treatment being carried out in the interests of work efficiency. A difficulty arises, however, when the employer is suspected of intruding on the employee's private life. This applies most clearly to the consumption of illicit drugs; many see drug testing of employees and subsequent referral for treatment as an infringement of civil liberties. This applies in principle to alcohol consumption, too.

Early and Family Intervention Programmes

Early intervention for alcohol problems has been mentioned several times in this book in connection with brief intervention programmes carried out in community settings and with the goal of reduced drinking. The interventions considered in this section are quite different. They are predicated on the disease concept of alcoholism, are aimed at total and lifelong abstinence, and involve the most subtle form of coercion considered here.

This approach begins with the identification of a concerned person who has a relative who may be drinking too much. Television advertisements may be used to reach such people, and they appeal to the notion of tough love to justify intervening without the drinker's consent. With the help of the concerned person, a group of people with various relationships to the drinker is then assembled, including perhaps spouse, children, other relatives, close friends, clergy, medical professionals or employers. These people are then persuaded to devise a plan to get the drinker into treatment and are coached in what to do and say if the drinker resists. Finally, if these efforts are successful, the drinker attends a facility that exists specifically to provide treatment for such clients and that initiated the plan to pressure them into seeking treatment. Numerous workshops in the United States teach this kind of intervention *(242)*.

Room *(240)* has explained that such active case-finding is linked to the entrepreneurial nature of the treatment system in the United States. Along with the expansion in treatment facilities came increased competition for customers between profit-making organizations with inpatient beds to fill. This is entirely different from the broadening of the base of interventions for alcohol problems that has been recommended in this book. In early and brief intervention, for example, the drinker should always be the target for advice and efforts to modify drinking. If the family or others who know the drinker are to be involved, this should only be done with his or her prior knowledge and full consent. In addition, except in cases of purely voluntary referral for serious alcohol problems, brief interventions are carried out in community settings, not specialized treatment facilities.

CHARACTERISTICS OF COERCED POPULATIONS

How do the people who are coerced into treatment compare with the general population and with the clinical population of problem drinkers who attend treatment on a voluntary basis? Research on this topic is fragmentary and incomplete *(242)* but some general conclusions are warranted.

First, people referred to programmes for drink-drivers or employee assistance – the two most prevalent kinds of coerced referrals in the United States – appear to have higher rates of alcohol problems than would be found in the general population. It is also true, however, that these problems are less numerous and severe than those of the typical clinical population. Thus, coercion does not in the main appear to involve people whose alcohol problems would be considered sufficiently serious for specialist treatment on a voluntary basis.

Drunkenness offenders are likely to have more severe alcohol problems than the two groups mentioned above. Nevertheless, the problems of homeless or vagrant people, who are often arrested for public drunkenness, extend far beyond alcohol. Many do not have a high level of alcohol dependence but suffer from various psychiatric disorders; their problems might well be seen as social or psychiatric. Compulsory treatment for alcoholism is often suspected to be merely a convenient means of disposing of people who are regarded as a nuisance.

OUTCOME OF COERCED TREATMENT

No matter the ethics of coerced treatment, one can ask whether it works. Once again, unfortunately, research on this topic is poor and largely inconclusive *(242)*.

The literature includes many reports of high success rates from employee assistance programmes, but these programmes are typically geared towards people with a good prognosis for treatment: high social stability, high levels of education and low degrees of dependence and alcohol-related problems. Indeed, the excellent chance of success among this population is precisely one of the arguments used in favour of the programmes.

Similar favourable indicators for treatment are found among people convicted of drink-driving, but the success of diversionary programmes for them is uncertain. Treatment seems clearly less effective in reducing the probability of re-offending than more overtly punitive measures such as licence suspensions *(251)*.

As mentioned in Chapter 9, Brewer *(121)* has claimed successful results for probation-linked disulfiram treatment for people with repeated convictions for drunkenness. Most of these offenders had shown several failures in treatment in the past and this is the main basis for the claim of successful outcome, rather than any controlled comparison with those who had not received court-mandated treatment. If the success of this form of coerced treatment is accepted, however, the ethics of the method still have to be debated.

In the absence of good evidence for or against the effectiveness of coerced treatment, we must return to basic principles for the likely success of treatment efforts. Much of what is known about the conditions under which successful treatment takes place – a full recognition of the problem, a commitment to the changes in lifestyle that abstinence or moderate drinking entails, and an acceptance of responsibility for bringing these changes about – make it unlikely that coerced treatment will be beneficial. At the very least, we may conclude that coerced referral to treatment whose effectiveness is largely unknown increases its ethical problems.

TREATMENT AND SOCIAL CONTROL

Another difficulty in deciding whether coerced treatment is successful is that the aims of such treatment are often unclear. In many instances, the primary objectives do not appear to be the health and welfare of the treated person but the wider interests of third parties, such as those of employers in improved work performance or of society in reduced crime. Fillmore & Kelso *(241)* have argued that the increased use of coerced treatment in the United States has transformed the social function of alcoholism treatment. Specifically, they say that it now tends to serve the interests of public order and social control rather than the welfare of the individual problem drinker.

This shift in emphasis must be seen in the context of the larger trend towards the medicalization of deviance that has occurred over the last 200 years *(248)*, in which behaviour that society finds troublesome is labelled as disease and controlled by branches of medicine rather than the legal system itself. The advantage to the state of such a definition is that, if something is seen as a disease and outside the individual's personal control, there can be little rational opposition to its enforced eradication. Latterly, however, criminological thought has reacted strongly against the confused understanding of treatment and punishment, and has attacked rehabilitation as an aim of the penal system *(252)*. Coerced referral to alcohol treatment may be one of the last bastions of a discredited social philosophy.

This is not to say that solving the issues linked to coercion and treatment is facile. As stated at the beginning of this chapter, coercion gives rise inevitably to difficult ethical dilemmas, particularly when it is sincerely believed to be in the best interests of the person coerced. We can conclude, however, that treatment providers should clearly separate in the mind the functions of social control and individual welfare, explicitly define and state the aims and objectives of treatment, and frankly acknowledge and debate the inherent ethical problems of coerced treatment.

15

A Comprehensive Treatment System

This final chapter considers how all the ingredients of the book can be put together to make up a comprehensive treatment service for problem drinkers. Describing this as an ideal treatment service would be tempting, but would be to go beyond the available evidence; we simply do not have enough high-quality information to know what the ideal treatment response should be. All that can be done is to use the existing evidence to arrive at a comprehensive service that is as rational, equitable and cost-effective as possible, and that attempts to serve the varying needs of all people with alcohol problems along with the needs of their families and society at large.

A basic assumption of this chapter is that one specialist agency cannot meet all these needs. This requires the combined efforts of a range of organizations and professional groups that encounter alcohol-related problems in their day-to-day work. The important task is to coordinate the activities of these different people to avoid waste and duplication and address all relevant needs. From this viewpoint, it is better to speak of a treatment system rather than merely a treatment service. An important property of a system is that changes in any of its component parts influence the activities of all the other parts. This underscores the need for coordination between all the different agencies in an area that come into contact with problem drinkers.

Describing an efficient treatment system that is applicable to a range of European countries presents formidable difficulties. The number and kinds of alcohol problems in each country may vary considerably, as do the baseline levels of treatment services for alcohol problems, psychiatric services and other related treatment facilities. Further, the different institutions that are relevant to the treatment system – such as various sorts of voluntary organizations, self-help groups or private treatment facilities, the organization of social services, and the operation of a criminal justice system – also show marked differences between countries. For these reasons, this chapter can only describe the broad principles that should underlie the develop-ment of comprehensive treatment systems; the operational specifica-tions of these principles and detailed configurations of services would depend on local arrangements, conventions and cultural conditions.

COMBINED VERSUS ALCOHOL-ONLY SERVICES

The discussion of one preliminary issue must precede the description of a comprehensive system: whether services for problem drinkers should be combined with those for people who use other drugs (illicit substances or medically prescribed drugs) or whether attention should be confined to alcohol. Each policy has advantages and disadvantages.

The main rationale for combined services is the fact of polydrug use. Although the proportion of polydrug users varies from country to country, their numbers have rapidly increased over the last 30 years or so in most parts of the world. In many countries, including highly industrialized societies, it is now comparatively rare to find someone whose harmful substance use is confined to alcohol. Without a combined service, therefore, the problems of polydrug users would either be shuttled back and forth between different agencies or partly ignored.

In addition, a combined service represents an economy of scale. Since similar kinds of treatment are often applied to substance use problems, it is sensible to bring together training and acquired expertise in one service. As this implies, the underlying justification for combined services is that the harmful use of dependence on different substances is due to the same kinds of fundamental processes and can be explained in similar theoretical terms. These different problems would therefore respond, in principle, to the same kinds of intervention. A combined service, it is argued, integrates theory and practice.

Against this, advocates of alcohol-only services argue that problem drinkers differ markedly from those who have problems with other drugs. The most obvious example of this is the age range, the mean age for problem drinkers in treatment being 35–40 years and that for illicit drug users 25–35 years. Problem drinkers also, it is claimed, have very different lifestyles, and the more "deviant" lifestyles and possible criminal involvement of illicit drug takers may put off the more "respectable" problem drinkers. This might deter problem drinkers from seeking help.

Another argument is that, despite a common explanation for addictive behaviour, illicit drug users need very different services, the prescribing of methadone being the obvious example. Finally, some argue that, in a combined service, the publicity given to illicit drugs would tend to swamp attention to alcohol problems and bias funding sources.

Since this book has so far dealt only with alcohol problems, this chapter follows suit and largely excludes the consideration of other drugs. Nevertheless, the persuasive arguments for combining alcohol and other drug services should be borne in mind. As in other areas, local circumstances must guide decision-making.

NEED ASSESSMENT

The long-term strategic planning of a treatment system for alcohol problems first requires assessment of the level and type of facilities needed for an adequate response to the relevant population. Need assessment is a general method for estimating the required capacity of treatment services on a local or regional level. It aims to determine how funds for the treatment of alcohol problems can be allocated to achieve the maximum benefit.

Kaelber & Nobel *(253)* have prepared an exhaustive review of need assessment methods employed in the United States. The majority of identified methods was based on demand; that is, service needs were projected on the basis of past patterns of use of treatment services as described by national data. The main limitation of this approach is that it does not specify how things ought to be, but merely reflects how they are. By contrast, a systems-based model projects services on the basis of what should be rather than what currently exists. This approach to need assessment takes account of research and informed opinion on the nature of and effective treatment for alcohol problems, and has the flexibility to change in the light of new research findings.

Rush *(254)* has described a model for system-based need assessment. In some ways this model is specific to the geographical area for which it was developed (Ontario, Canada) but many of its concepts and assumptions have a wider application. One assumption is that each treatment system should consist of a number of components that together make up a continuum of care – from health promotion to long-term rehabilitation – for responding to alcohol problems of all types and degrees of severity. The immediate aim of the systems approach is to estimate how much of each treatment component is required per population unit. The wider aim is to maximize the degree of overlap between the need, the demand and the supply of services within available resources.

Godfrey et al. *(255)* have also described a systems-based need assessment approach, based partly on Rush's model. This approach has seven steps:

1. defining the geographic area;
2. estimating the size and composition of the population in need;
3. describing the desired system of services;
4. assessing current provision;
5. estimating the demand for each type of service;
6. comparing the preferred to the current demands for each service and devising the means of changing the pattern of services towards the preferred provision; and
7. devising instruments to monitor and evaluate changes and to revise the need assessment.

1. As a first step in calculating the size of the population in need, the interested parties must agree on the geographical boundaries of the area to be covered. Larger areas usually provide more varied and useful sources of data.

2. The number of problem drinkers at each level of severity in the area should be estimated. The families of those with severe problems are likely to be adversely affected and need help, and should be included in the calculation. Data should be collected on the number of problem drinkers, the types of alcohol-related problems and levels of consumption.

Existing information is likely to be limited and can be supplemented by three methods, depending on the resources available and current data sources: direct measurement of consumption and problems by randomized surveys of the local population, reasonable extrapolation from national or regional surveys of drinking and problems, and indirect use of indicators such as rates of liver cirrhosis or drink-driving offences. A three-way categorization of problem drinkers that could be used as a basis for this step is given below.

3. Describing the desired system of services clearly depends on the availability of resources, both financial and human, in the area in question. Also, one treatment system is unlikely to fit the needs of all areas within a country, given the differences in local priorities and existing facilities. The balance of service provision and funding between health and social care organizations is of particular concern, and consideration should be given to factors that affect how and when problem drinkers present to both generalist and specialist services. Efficient assessment and referral procedures are needed to ensure that the needs of those seeking help are matched to the most appropriate services, and various models exist for this purpose *(255)*. The desired system should ensure adequate coverage for men and women, and groups of different ages, ethnic backgrounds and special needs, as well as different kinds of alcohol problem (see Introduction).

The following section lists the possible components of a comprehensive treatment system. Normally, however, both fund holders and service providers should take part in prioritizing service needs. There must be an attempt to persuade agencies with different care philosophies and professional priorities, which may see themselves as competitors, to work together for the common good.

4. In the assessment of current service provision, information about organizations offering services to residents of a local area, the types of treatment they offer and how assessments and referrals are made may be patchy and poorly integrated. Heads of organizations and other key informants from among those dealing with alcohol problems should be surveyed to provide information on current services and to identify gaps in service provision. This information can be updated and improved in various ways.

5. Estimating the demand for each type of service means trying to predict the proportion of the population in need that will present for and could receive each of the components of the desired treatment system. Such estimates, however, will probably be based on very limited information. Basic decisions are required to determine how many members of the total population in need will be offered intervention in any year. This will depend on the treatment system adopted, the resources available, the willingness of problem drinkers to present to different components of the treatment system, and the priorities negotiated between interested parties.

6. The preferred and the current demands for each service should be compared, and means devised to shift the pattern of services towards the former. This is a long-term objective and several cycles of planning and implementation must pass before system-based need assessment can be fully implemented. If the essential first steps of measuring the population in need and assessing current service provision are taken, however, the necessary changes can gradually be made.

7. Instruments should be devised to monitor and evaluate changes and to revise the need assessment. This final step is necessary to ensure progress in service provision. Godfrey et al. *(255)* give details.

PRINCIPLES OF THE TREATMENT SYSTEM

The previous section identified the delineation of a desired system of services as an essential part of need assessment. Of course, the features of such a system would inevitably vary between countries. This is because of differences in existing arrangements, the organizational relationships between relevant sectors of government, and the traditions and principles determining the response to alcohol problems, as well as a host of other reasons. Perhaps the best analogy is to say that what can be described here are the essential ingredients for a recipe; how and in what proportions they are mixed is largely a matter for each country. To extend the analogy, different areas within each country are likely to require treatment systems with different emphases to accommodate local factors; systems would have the same ingredients, but take on a different shape and appearance in each locality.

Several basic principles should underlie the desired treatment system. The foremost reflects a constant theme of this book: the need to broaden the base of the treatment response. Two factors give rise to this need:

- the widening of attention from an exclusive preoccupation with severe alcohol dependence and problems to a cognizance of the complete range of problems of a less severe nature, which account for the majority of alcohol problems in society; and
- the fact that many different professional groups encounter problem drinkers in their day-to day work and must therefore be regarded as a crucial aspect of the treatment system.

The other principles underlying the treatment system are obvious but worth emphasizing. By definition, the system must be a planned and integrated local response to alcohol problems, not fragmentary, disconnected and uncoordinated. The system and its individual parts must be accountable and their performance measurable by objective criteria. They must also be flexible enough to change in response to the changing needs of the local population and fresh developments in scientific knowledge and treatment technology.

Edwards & Unnithal *(256)* have recently described a model for a desired treatment system. The present recommendations follow their model, but with some important differences in emphasis. The continuum of care mentioned in the previous section can be broken down into services for three categories of problem drinker.

Type I problem drinkers comprise the excessive drinkers with no or few alcohol-related problems and low levels of dependence. This category corresponds roughly with the "hazardous drinkers" mentioned in Chapter 1. They drink at levels over medically recommended limits for low-risk drinking but have either avoided significant alcohol-related problems or failed to recognize them. They certainly do not seek help for any such problems. While most people in this category show some evidence of alcohol dependence – even if only a raised tolerance for alcohol effects or an increased importance of drinking in the lifestyle – their level of dependence is low as measured by standard instruments (see Chapter 3).

Type II problem drinkers comprise those with definite alcohol-related problems but only moderate levels of dependence. This category includes most of the people who recognize that they have a problem with drinking, even if this recognition has only come about reluctantly, through pressure from family members, employers or others. These drinkers, however, do not have a high level of dependence, and have probably not reached the stage of relief drinking (drinking to abolish or avoid withdrawal symptoms). This is a very large category and includes people with problems that vary widely in type and seriousness. Nevertheless, in older terminology, individuals in this category would probably not have been described as chronic alcoholics.

Type III problem drinkers comprise those with definite alcohol-related problems and severe dependence. These people would, in older language, have been described as chronic alcoholics. Many have serious and long-standing problems. They have typically experienced significant alcohol withdrawal and formed the habit of drinking to counter incipient withdrawal symptoms. Many have had several or numerous previous episodes of treatment.

How can the needs of these three categories of problem drinker be met? The treatment system can be seen as divided into three integrated parts: specialist services, generalist services linked to an alcohol liaison team, and a coordinating mechanism.

SPECIALIST SERVICES

Specialist services are required for many type II and all type III problem drinkers. The staff should have special knowledge and expertise in the field of alcohol problems and dependence (or addictive behaviour in general) and have received some form of specialized training in the treatment of alcohol problems. The mixture of disciplines can vary, and include psychiatrists, gastroenterologists (or other types of physician with a special interest in alcohol problems), clinical psychologists, nurses, social workers, occupational therapists and counsellors of no particular professional affiliation. The exact mix must depend on the types of training and expertise available in each country and other local factors. Seven types of specialized service would normally be required.

Assessment and Referral Service

Some central agency should be responsible for formally assessing the treatment needs of type II and type III problem drinkers, and determining the form of detoxification (if any) and treatment (including setting, intensity and favoured modality) that should be offered them (see Chapter 3). The service would receive referrals from local GPs, social workers, probation officers and other community agents, and would make referrals to other facilities when appropriate. Part of the remit of the alcohol liaison team (see below) would be to educate local agencies on the circumstances when a referral to the centre is warranted and when they should consider intervening themselves, with support from the liaison team.

The assessment service should not be perceived as an ivory tower, remote from the community it is supposed to serve. Assessment should therefore take place on an outreach basis.

Another important function of the assessment service is to arrange for case management for each client, to ensure continuity of support during the client's contact with the various agencies that might be involved in the treatment response. This requires the nomination of a key worker who would take overall responsibility for the progress of an individual client through the treatment system. Ogborne & Rush *(257)* have described and reviewed the roles of assessment and referral centres in the addictions field.

Detoxification Service

As suggested in Chapter 2, most detoxification can take place in the community, either on an outpatient basis or at the client's home. In the latter case, the alcohol liaison team (see below) should have a role in training and supporting detoxification supervised by GPs. A non-medicated, inpatient detoxification facility would be an alternative for some clients. No matter which type of detoxification is used, efforts should be made to ensure continuity with treatment proper.

A Small Inpatient Unit

This book has established that as a general response to problem drinking, inpatient treatment is highly cost-ineffective and should largely give way to non-residential forms of treatment (see Chapter 6). Nevertheless, a relatively small number of inpatient places should probably be retained for the few people with particularly severe and complex problems who seem likely to benefit from a temporary break from the outside world. These would almost always be type III problem drinkers. A few clients with evidence of physical or psychological co-morbidity would need to be referred to medical or psychiatric inpatient care, unless the conditions could conveniently be treated in the alcohol inpatient unit. In addition, people who could be expected to experience a severe and possibly life-threatening withdrawal syndrome would need to be detoxified on a medicated, inpatient basis (Chapter 2). Those who have failed community-based detoxification should also be considered for admission.

Outpatient Treatment and Counselling Service

Outpatient treatment and counselling should comprise the bulk of the treatment offered to type II and many type III problem drinkers, after detoxification or when suitable accommodation has been arranged. This should be the main component of the specialist treatment response. The effective treatment approaches described in this book, matched on rational grounds to the client's particular problems and characteristics, should form the basis of outpatient treatment.

Many of the problem drinkers in question, especially those of type II, would not need a lengthy and protracted outpatient programme. Some clients' problems would be sufficiently serious or complicated by psychological or social factors as to indicate an immediate and intensive outpatient programme. In most cases, however, and certainly for the great majority of those receiving treatment for the first time, offering a relatively brief intervention (four or fewer sessions), at least as a first step in treatment, would be best. Both research evidence and the need for the cost-effective use of resources justify such a policy. If the client does not respond to a brief intervention, the intensity of treatment can be increased. Sobell & Sobell *(258)* have recently described a "stepped care" model of treatment along these lines (Fig. 7).

Fig. 7. Stepped care model of treatment for alcohol problems

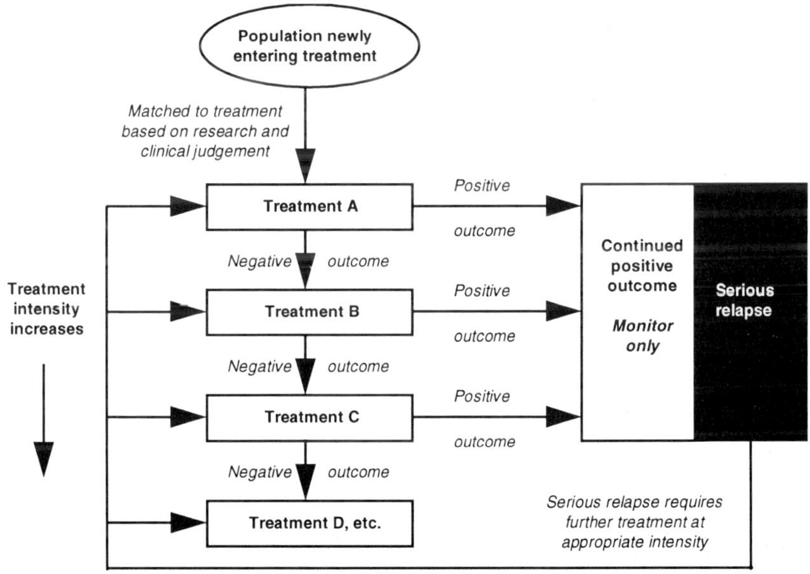

Source: Sobell & Sobell *(258)*.

As the stepped care model implies, an efficient system of treatment, follow-up and aftercare (see Chapter 11) is a highly desirable accompaniment to an outpatient service, or indeed to any specialist treatment facility. In addition, a proportion of clients of the outpatient service, normally some of those in type II, should initially be offered a moderation goal if they prefer it to abstinence. If more intensive treatment becomes necessary, the goal of treatment can be renegotiated and changed to abstinence (see Chapter 5).

The location of the outpatient service is an important consideration, in view of the need to make it accessible. The best location is a central site in the community that clients can easily reach. The service should not be situated in a general or psychiatric hospital, owing to the stigma of illness that arises from such a location. The assessment and referral service, the detoxification service, the small inpatient unit, the outpatient clinic and the day treatment facility would normally be located at the same site.

Day Treatment Facility

In addition to the outpatient service, a day treatment service can also be offered, resources permitting. Such a service would typically operate for five days a week for three or four hours per day. The facility can serve two types of function:

- to structure the day for unemployed clients who may need advice on housing requirements, welfare entitlements or opportunities for work, with the possible involvement of generic social services; and
- to provide specific treatment programmes, probably on a group basis and involving skills training and other cognitive–behavioural methods (see Chapter 11).

Hostel Facilities

Hostel facilities are obviously necessary for the rehabilitation of homeless problem drinkers. Voluntary agencies often own and run hostels but, whatever their provenance, hostel activities must be integrated with those of the other services and with local authority housing policy.

Separate Services for Young People and Women

There is a strong argument for separating treatment for young problem drinkers (those under 21 years of age) from regular treatment facilities. Many such young people are polydrug users and the justification for combined drug services is perhaps more pressing here. The need for a separate service for young people gains urgency from the growing number of teenagers in many parts of the world who have problems with alcohol and/or illicit drugs.

There is also an argument for offering separate facilities to female problem drinkers, especially those with young children who need crèche facilities. The evidence *(259)* suggests that women-only services attract clients who would not otherwise attend for treatment. Even if separate facilities are not established, women's different service needs should be recognized.

GENERALIST SERVICES AND THE ALCOHOL LIAISON TEAM

In addition to specialist services, any modern, comprehensive treatment system must include well resourced support for efforts to reduce and prevent problem drinking in the wider community. This component of the comprehensive service is geared to the needs of all type I problem drinkers and some of those in type II. Although conceptually distinct, the alcohol liaison team should have an organizational link to the specialist services in order to draw upon their expertise. The main functions of the alcohol liaison team are as follows.

Training and Support

The main role of the alcohol liaison team is to train and support a variety of professional groups in the delivery of opportunistic brief interventions (see Chapters 6 and 7) to hazardous and problem drinkers whom they encounter in their day-to-day work. These training efforts can make use of packages that have been specially developed for this purpose. The team should encourage community agents to use brief intervention packages by educating them about alcohol-related damage and the important role that they can play in combating it, assist in the efficient implementation of screening and brief interventions, and ensure that brief interventions continue to be used. The modification of the style of intervention – from confrontation or prescription to the negotiation of behavioural change *(260)* – is also an important part of the alcohol liaison team's educational work. As mentioned above, community agents also need to understand when to refer clients to specialist facilities.

Sometimes more than a brief intervention may be needed, and the community agent may be able and willing to take this on. The team should not normally discourage this, but it may need to give expert advice and support. Further, in some circumstances – for example, a patient with a primary psychiatric disorder who also has an alcohol problem – advice on aspects of the case would be needed from members of the alcohol liaison team. Finally, team members should not demur from directly carrying out treatment or counselling at a general medical practice, for example, when reasonably requested to do so.

Community-based Assessments

The alcohol liaison team should conduct assessments at various locations in the community for problem drinkers of types II and III, when requested to do so. These assessments should follow the protocols used in the central assessment service and should result in the same range of treatment decisions.

Health Education and Promotion

Although this book is concerned with the treatment of alcohol problems, the distinction between treatment and prevention is ultimately artificial and preventive work should be an essential part of the alcohol liaison team's activities. If not carried out alongside a comprehensive treatment system, such preventive work would probably not be done at all. Health education on high-risk drinking and health promotion that includes advice on alcohol consumption can be carried out in schools, workplaces and other community settings, as well as being aimed at special groups (such as ethnic groups at high risk for alcohol problems) and the general population. Special events can be infrequently but regularly organized to publicize this work.

In addition to the more general attempt to raise the level of community awareness of harmful alcohol use through education, the alcohol liaison team could take more specific measures. These could include opposing unnecessary new outlets for alcohol sales or consumption, attempting to ensure the enforcement of laws against underage drinking or the serving of intoxicated people, and organizing community objections to unethical alcohol advertisements. Tether & Robinson *(261)* give a guide to local action to prevent alcohol problems.

Settings for the Team's Work

A list of the professional groups and settings that should be incorporated into the remit of the alcohol liaison team may assist thinking about the team's work.

General Practice

General medical practice is the most important setting and professional group for team involvement. In most countries, a high proportion of the population visits a GP each year, and the GP remains a source of prestige and authority in the community. GPs usually have a knowledge of the whole family situation that is often helpful in an effective intervention. Moreover, under an expanded definition of an alcohol problem, specialist services can never be sufficient to meet the need. For these reasons, much of the national response to alcohol damage, particularly early intervention and secondary prevention, must rely on the efforts of GPs. This represents the most cost-effective single policy for the reduction of alcohol problems in any society.

As already indicated, the main thrust of the effort to involve GPs relies on the concept of brief intervention, and the evidence reviewed (Chapter 7) shows that such interventions can be highly effective. As suggested, some GPs may wish to take on the treatment of more severe cases and the alcohol liaison team should assist them to do so. Finally, the team should encourage and support GPs to supervise detoxification if severe withdrawal is not expected.

The Hospital

Another fertile field for early intervention among problem drinkers is the general hospital ward. The evidence suggests that 20–40% of male patients on many types of ward drink at levels above those medically recommended *(262)*. Physicians and nurses should be encouraged and supported to include screening and intervention in their normal duties.

Accident and emergency departments often require specialized advice and help in the management of problem drinkers, and they are a potentially important setting for early intervention. In addition to brief intervention work, the alcohol liaison team should regularly provide consultation and advice to some types of hospital ward, such as gastrointestinal or orthopaedic wards, in which an unusually high proportion of problem drinkers can be expected to present. Further, maternal and child services need special kinds of input and advice.

Social Work

The social damage from harmful drinking may be as pervasive and undesirable as the damage to health. Social workers who often encounter clients with alcohol problems need advice, support and training, particularly with respect to such matters as the involvement of excessive drinking in child and spouse abuse.

The Criminal Justice System

The same considerations apply to the work of probation officers. In addition, many prisoners in penal institutions show problems with drinking, and a significant number would not have offended were it not for their dependence on alcohol or intoxication patterns. Pre-release interventions for prisoners, supported by continued attention following release, have been insufficiently explored and should be included within the remit of the alcohol liaison team. Drink-drivers are an obvious source of candidates for early intervention programmes.

The Workplace

The alcohol liaison team should persuade employers in the private and public sectors to institute workplace policies on alcohol, including a complete ban on alcohol consumption at work for all levels of staff. Alcohol should become a central topic in workplace health promotion activities, and special provision should be made to identify and help the employees more seriously affected by their drinking.

Special Client Categories

The possible need for units to deal specifically with the alcohol problems of young people and women has already been mentioned. Both the alcohol liaison team and the specialist services, however, should plan for a number of other special categories of client (see Introduction). For example, communities with minority ethnic groups would need workers who know the ethnic groups' languages and understand their cultures.

In addition, problem drinkers who are elderly or disabled have special problems and needs. As already indicated, attention should be paid to the needs of families of problem drinkers, especially of those with long-standing and severe problems.

One group requiring particular attention comprises people with cognitive impairment resulting from excessive alcohol consumption. Depending on their numbers among the population in need, a special unit may need to be set up for the treatment of clients with alcohol-related brain damage. In any event, the special difficulties of treatment and rehabilitation for such clients should be remembered.

Finally, as already noted, many problem drinkers show problems with other psychoactive substances. If services are not combined, the effects of other substances on clients' welfare and treatment outcome must not be overlooked. The alcohol liaison team would need to establish close working relationships with agencies responsible for dealing with other types of harmful substance use.

A COORDINATING MECHANISM

The final element of a comprehensive system for the treatment of alcohol problems is some means of knitting together all the listed components to coordinate their activities and avoid fragmentation and duplication. This would usually be the task of a local alcohol coordinating committee, which should meet on a regular basis and include among its members representatives of all the various arms of the treatment system and relevant funding agencies.

The coordinating committee would normally commission the need assessment mentioned earlier in this chapter, and its major function would be to oversee the efficient implementation of the strategic plan for treatment services that is developed. The committee would therefore monitor and coordinate the activities of the statutory bodies described above that make up the main treatment response. Equally important would be the coordination of other, non-statutory agencies involved in the field of alcohol problems. These include voluntary and charitable bodies, self-help groups such as AA, and private, profit-making facilities.

The practical operation of a committee of this sort – for example, what kind of person should chair it and where it should stand in relation to other decision-making bodies – cannot be discussed here. This must depend on the particular traditions and circumstances of the country and local community. Nevertheless, representatives of other interested parties – such as the police, the courts, social work, local business, trade unions and religious organizations – would normally be included on the committee.

The service requirements that the committee would need to coordinate may seem overwhelming. This is because of the huge scale and pervasiveness of alcohol problems in most societies and communities. As previously made clear, current resources may not permit the implementation of all these aspects of the treatment system. Such a situation necessitates difficult choices among competing priorities.

EVALUATION AND RESEARCH

A description of a comprehensive treatment system would be incomplete without the mention of evaluation and research, which should be seen as essential components of the system. Evaluation should include the continuing monitoring of the performance of the treatment system and the identification of ways to improve or modify it to meet changing circumstances.

Important here are the setting of objective and reasonable criteria for judging the efficiency of the system in meeting its goals, and the identification of specific indicators for determining whether such criteria have been met. These indicators should not describe the effectiveness of interventions only in terms of their success rates, although this would obviously be a crucial aspect of performance. Other important aspects, however, include the ability of the service to reach the population in need and its equity in providing necessary help to all sections of the community, including disadvantaged groups. Community-wide indicators, such as average consumption levels, local rates of liver cirrhosis and drink-driving offences, should ideally be collected from time to time to see if the treatment system is having the intended effect on the health and welfare of the entire community.

In addition, a properly designed system should always set aside some its resources for basic and applied research on the prevention and treatment of alcohol problems. As well as contributing to national and international efforts to understand and reduce problem drinking, this would have the more immediate benefit of raising the intellectual level of the service staff. This would increase the likelihood that they would recognize and incorporate improvements into the treatment system.

References

1. MILLER, W.R. & HESTER, R.K. The effectiveness of alcoholism treatment: what research reveals. *In*: Miller, W.R. & Heather, N., ed. *Treating addictive behaviors: processes of change.* New York, Plenum, 1986.
2. INSTITUTE OF MEDICINE. *Prevention and treatment of alcohol problems: research opportunities.* Washington, DC, National Academy Press, 1989.
3. INSTITUTE OF MEDICINE. *Broadening the base of treatment for alcohol problems.* Washington, DC, National Academy Press, 1990.
4. HOLDER, H. ET AL. The cost effectiveness of treatment for alcoholism: a first approximation. *Journal of studies on alcohol*, **52**: 517–540 (1991).
5. MATTICK, R.P. & JARVIS, T., ED. *An outline for the management of alcohol problems: quality assurance project.* Canberra, Australian Government Publishing Service, 1993 (National Drug Strategy Monograph Series, No. 20).
6. THOM, B. & FRANEY, C. *Alcohol treatment since 1983: a review of the research literature. Report to the Alcohol Education and Research Council.* London, Centre for Research on Drugs and Health Behaviour, 1994.
7. EDWARDS, G. *The treatment of drinking problems: a guide for the helping professions.* London, Grant McIntyre, 1982.
8. MARLATT, G.A. & GORDON, J.R. *Relapse prevention: maintenance strategies in the treatment of addictive behaviors.* New York, Guilford, 1985.
9. COX, W.M., ED. *Treatment and prevention of alcohol problems: a resource manual.* New York, Academic Press, 1987.

10. Hester, R.K. & Miller, W.R., ed. *Handbook of alcoholism treatment approaches: effective alternatives.* New York, Pergamon, 1989.
11. Monti, P.M. et al. *Treating alcohol dependence.* New York, Guilford, 1989.
12. Miller, W.R. & Rollnick, S. *Motivational interviewing: preparing people to change addictive behavior.* New York, Guilford, 1991.
13. O'Farrell, T.J., ed. *Treating alcohol problems: marital and family interventions.* New York, Guilford, 1993.
14. Jarvis, T.J. et al. *Treatment approaches for alcohol and drug dependence: an introductory guide.* Chichester, John Wiley & Sons, 1995.
15. Heather, N. & Robertson, I. *Problem drinking*, 2nd ed. Oxford, Oxford University Press, 1989.
16. Cahalan, D. *Problem drinkers: a national survey.* San Francisco, Jossey-Bass, 1970.
17. Fillmore, K.M. Prevalence, incidence and chronicity of drinking patterns and problems among men as a function of age: a longitudinal and cohort analysis. *British journal of addiction*, **82**: 77–83 (1987).
18. Kreitman, N. Alcohol consumption and the preventive paradox. *British journal of addiction*, **81**: 353–363 (1986).
19. Edwards, G. et al. *Alcohol policy and the public good.* Oxford, Oxford University Press, 1995.
20. Edwards, G. et al. Nomenclature and classification of drug- and alcohol-related problems: a shortened version of a WHO memorandum. *British journal of addiction*, **77**: 3–20 (1982).
21. Edwards, G. & Gross, M. Alcohol dependence: provisional description of a clinical syndrome. *British medical journal*: **281**: 1058–1061 (1976).
22. American Psychiatric Association. *Diagnostic and statistical manual of mental disorders*, 4th ed. Washington, DC, American Psychiatric Association, 1994.
23. *The ICD-10 classification of mental and behavioural disorders: clinical descriptions and diagnostic guidelines.* Geneva, World Health Organization, 1992.
24. Alterman, A.I. et al. Treatment response and safety of ambulatory medical detoxification. *Journal of studies on alcohol*, **49**: 160–166 (1988).

25. STOCKWELL, T. ET AL. Home detoxification for problem drinkers: acceptability to clients, relatives, general practitioners and outcome after 60 days. *British journal of addiction*, **85**: 61–70 (1990).
26. STOCKWELL, T. The Exeter home detoxification project. *In:* Stockwell, T. & Clement, S., ed. *Helping the problem drinker: new initiatives in community care.* London, Croom Helm, 1987.
27. SPARADEO, F.R. ET AL. Evaluation of a social-setting detoxification program. *Journal of studies on alcohol*, **43**: 1124–1136 (1982).
28. SAUNDERS, J.B. Drug treatment in alcoholism. *In:* Burrows, G.D. et al., ed. *Drugs in psychiatry*. New York, Elsevier, 1987, Vol. 4.
29. SHAW, J.M. ET AL. Development of optimal treatment tactics for alcohol withdrawal. I: assessment and effectiveness of supportive care. *Journal of clinical pharmacology*, **1**: 382–389 (1981).
30. HAYASHIDA, M. ET AL. Comparative effectiveness and costs of inpatient and outpatient detoxification of patients with mild-to-moderate alcohol withdrawal syndrome. *New England journal of medicine*, **320**: 358–365 (1989).
31. SAUNDERS, J.B. ET AL. Development of the Alcohol Use Disorders Identification Screening Test (AUDIT). WHO collaborative project on early detection of persons with harmful alcohol consumption – II. *Addiction*, **88**: 791–804 (1993).
32. SUTHERLAND, G. ET AL. The impact of a research interview on clinical re-attendance: a happy finding. *British journal of addiction*, **80**: 211–212 (1985).
33. SKINNER, H.A. & ALLEN, B.A. Does the computer make a difference? Computerized versus face-to-face versus self-report assessment of alcohol, drug and tobacco use. *Journal of consulting and clinical psychology*, **51**: 267–275 (1983).
34. LETTIERI, D.J. ET AL., ED. *Alcoholism treatment assessment research instruments.* Washington, DC, US Government Printing Office, 1985.
35. LITTEN, R.Z. & ALLEN, J.P., ED. *Measuring alcohol consumption: psychosocial and biochemical methods.* Totowa, NJ, Humana Press, 1992.

36. SOBELL, L.C. ET AL. Reliability of a timeline method: assessing normal drinkers' reports of recent drinking and comparative evaluation across several populations. *British journal of addiction*, **83**: 393–402 (1988).
37. MILLER, W.R. & MARLATT, G.A. *Manual for the comprehensive drinker profile.* Odessa, FL, Psychological Assessment Resources Inc., 1984.
38. SKINNER, H.A. *Development and validation of a lifetime alcohol consumption assessment procedure.* Toronto, Addiction Research Foundation, 1982.
39. WHELAN, G. Biological markers of alcoholism. *Australian and New Zealand journal of medicine*, **22**: 209–213 (1992).
40. DAVIDSON, R. Assessment of the alcohol dependence syndrome: a review of self-reporting screening questionnaires. *British journal of clinical psychology*, **26**: 243–255 (1987).
41. STOCKWELL, T.R. ET AL. The development of a questionnaire to measure severity of alcohol dependence. *British journal of addiction*, **74**: 79–87 (1979).
42. STOCKWELL, T. ET AL. The measurement of alcohol dependence and impaired control in community samples. *Addiction*, **89**: 176–184 (1994).
43. SKINNER, H.A. & ALLEN, B.A. Alcohol dependence syndrome, measurement and validation. *Journal of abnormal psychology*, **91**: 199–209 (1982).
44. RAISTRICK, D. ET AL. Development of a questionnaire to measure alcohol dependence. *British journal of addiction*, **78**: 89–95 (1983).
45. DRUMMOND, D.C. The relationship between alcohol dependence and alcohol-related problems in a clinical population. *British journal of addiction*, **85**: 357–366 (1990).
46. MCCONNAUGHY, E.A. ET AL. Stages of change in psychotherapy: measurement and sample profiles. *Psychotherapy: theory, research and practice*, **20**: 368–375 (1983).
47. PROCHASKA, J.O. & DICLEMENTE, C.C. Stages of change in the modification of problem behaviors. *In:* Hersen, M. et al., ed. *Progress in behavior modification.* Newbury Park, CA, Sage, 1992.

48. ROLLNICK, S. ET AL. Development of a short readiness to change questionnaire for use in brief, opportunistic interventions among excessive drinkers. *British journal of addiction*, **87**: 743–754 (1992).
49. ANNIS, H.M. ET AL. *Inventory of drinking situations: users' guide.* Toronto, Addiction Research Foundation, 1987.
50. ANNIS, H.M. & GRAHAM, J.M. *Situational confidence questionnaire (SCQ): users' guide.* Toronto, Addiction Research Foundation, 1988.
51. CHANEY, E.F. ET AL. Skill training with alcoholics. *Journal of consulting and clinical psychology*, **46**: 1092–1104 (1978).
52. GOLDBERG, D.P. *The detection of psychiatric illness by questionnaire.* Oxford, Oxford University Press, 1972.
53. WILKINSON, D.A. & SANCHEZ-CRAIG, M. Relevance of brain dysfunction to treatment objectives: should alcohol-related cognitive deficits influence the way we think about treatment? *Addictive behaviors*, **6**: 253–260 (1981).
54. CORNEY, R.H. & CLARE, A.W. The construction, development and testing of a self-report questionnaire to identify social problems. *Psychological medicine*, **15**: 637–649 (1985).
55. O'FARRELL, T.J. & MAISTO, S.A. The utility of self-report and biological measures of alcohol consumption in alcoholism treatment outcome studies. *Advances in behaviour research and therapy*, **9**: 91–125 (1987).
56. HOLT, L. ET AL. Early identification of alcohol abuse: 2. Clinical and laboratory indicators. *Canadian Medical Association journal*, **124**: 1279–1295 (1981).
57. ANNIS, H.M. & SANCHEZ-CRAIG, M. "Self-monitoring" and "recall" measures of alcohol consumption: convergent validity with biochemical indices of liver function. *British journal on alcohol and alcoholism*, **17**: 117–121 (1982).
58. GLASER, F.B. Anybody got a match? Treatment research and the matching hypothesis. *In:* Edwards, G. & Grant, M., ed. *Alcoholism treatment in transition.* London, Croom Helm, 1980.
59. GOTTHEIL, E. ET AL., ED. *Matching patient needs and treatment methods in alcoholism and drug abuse.* Springfield, IL, Charles C. Thomas, 1981.

60. FINNEY, J.W. & MOOS, R.H. Matching patients with treatments: conceptual and methodological issues. *Journal of studies on alcohol*, **47**: 122–134 (1986).
61. MILLER, W.R. & HESTER, R.K. Matching problem drinkers with optimal treatments. *In:* Miller, W.R. & Heather, N., ed. *Treating addictive behaviors: processes of change.* New York, Plenum, 1986.
62. MILLER, W.R. Matching individuals with interventions. *In:* Hester, R.K. & Miller, W.R., ed. *Handbook of alcoholism treatment approaches: effective alternatives.* New York, Pergamon, 1989.
63. LINDSTROM, L. *Managing alcoholism: matching clients to treatments.* Oxford, Oxford University Press, 1992.
64. ANNIS, H.M. & CHAN, D. The differential treatment model: empirical evidence from a personality typology. *Criminal justice and behavior*, **10**: 159–173 (1983).
65. MCLELLAN, A.T. ET AL. Matching substance abuse patients to appropriate treatment methods: a conceptual and methodological approach. *Journal of nervous and mental diseases*, **171**: 597–605 (1983).
66. KADDEN, R.M. ET AL. Matching alcoholics to coping skills or interactional therapies: post-treatment results. *Journal of consulting and clinical psychology*, **57**: 698–704 (1990).
67. HAMBURG, S. Behavior therapy in alcoholism: a critical review of broad spectrum approaches. *Journal of studies on alcohol*, **36**: 69–87 (1975).
68. MCLACHLAN, J.F.C. Benefit from group therapy as a function of patient–therapist match on conceptual level. *Psychotherapy: theory, research and practice*, **9**: 317–323 (1972).
69. EWING, J.A. Matching therapy and patients: the cafeteria plan. *British journal of addiction*, **72**: 13–18 (1977).
70. KISSIN, B. ET AL. Social and psychological factors in the treatment of chronic alcoholism. *Journal of psychiatric research*, **8**: 13–27 (1970).
71. PATTISON, E.M. ET AL. Abstinence and normal drinking: an assessment of changes in drinking patterns in alcoholics after treatment. *Quarterly journal of studies on alcohol*, **29**: 610–633 (1968).

72. HEATHER, N. & ROBERTSON, I. *Controlled drinking*. London, Methuen, 1983.
73. HEATHER, N. Misleading confusion. *British journal of addiction*, **82**: 253–255 (1987).
74. ORFORD, J. & KEDDIE, A. Abstinence or controlled drinking in clinical practice: a test of the dependence and persuasion hypotheses. *British journal of addiction*, **81**: 495–504 (1986).
75. ELAL-LAWRENCE, G. ET AL. Predictors of outcome type in treated problem drinkers. *Journal of studies on alcohol*, **47**: 41–47 (1986).
76. HEATHER, N. Brief intervention strategies. *In:* Hester, R.K. & Miller, W.R., ed. *Handbook of alcoholism treatment approaches: effective alternatives,* 2nd ed. Needham Heights, MA, Allyn & Bacon, 1995.
77. POLICH, J.M. ET AL. *The course of alcoholism: four years after treatment.* Santa Monica, CA, Rand Corporation, 1980.
78. PATTISON, E.M. A conceptual approach to alcoholism treatment goals. *Addictive behaviors*, **1**: 177–192 (1976).
79. HEATHER, N. The application of harm reduction principles to the treatment of alcohol problems. *In:* Heather, N. et al., ed. *Psychoactive drugs and harm reduction: from faith to science.* London, Whurr, 1993.
80. GOTTHEIL, E. ET AL. Follow-up of abstinent and non-abstinent alcoholics. *American journal of psychiatry*, **139**: 560–565 (1982).
81. HEATHER, N. & TEBBUTT, J. Definitions of non-abstinent and abstinent categories in alcoholism treatment outcome classifications: a review and proposal. *Drug and alcohol dependence*, **24**: 83–93 (1989).
82. MILLER, W.R. & HESTER, R.K. Inpatient alcoholism treatment: who benefits? *American psychologist*, **41**: 794–805 (1986).
83. ANNIS, H.M. Is inpatient rehabilitation of the alcoholic cost-effective? Con position. *Advances in alcohol and substance abuse*, **5**: 175–190 (1987).
84. HEATHER, N. Relationships between delinquency and drunkenness among Scottish young offenders. *British journal on alcohol and alcoholism*, **16**: 50–61 (1981).
85. RICHMOND, R. ET AL. *Workplace policies and programmes for tobacco, alcohol and other drugs in Australia.* Canberra,

Australian Government Printing Office, 1992 (NCADA Monograph Series, No. 24).

86. DRUMMOND, D.C. ET AL. Specialist versus general practitioner treatment of problem drinkers. *Lancet*, **336**: 915–918 (1990).

87. HEATHER, N. ET AL. Evaluation of a self-help manual for media-recruited problem drinkers: six month follow-up results. *British journal of clinical psychology*, **25**: 19–34 (1986).

88. HEATHER, N. ET AL. Assisted natural recovery from alcohol problems: effects of a self-help manual with and without supplementary telephone contact. *British journal of addiction*, **85**: 1177–1185 (1990).

89. ORFORD, J. & EDWARDS, G. *Alcoholism: a comparison of treatment and advice with a study of the influence of marriage*. Oxford, Oxford University Press, 1977 (Maudsley Monographs, No. 26).

90. EDWARDS, G. ET AL. What happens to alcoholics? *Lancet*, **2**(8344): 269–271 (1983).

91. RUSSELL, M. ET AL. Effect of general practitioners' advice against smoking. *British medical journal*, **284**: 231–236 (1979).

92. WALLACE, P. ET AL. Randomized controlled trial of general practitioner intervention in patients with excessive alcohol consumption. *British medical journal*, **297**: 663–668 (1988).

93. ANDERSON, P. & SCOTT, E. The effect of general practitioners' advice to heavy drinking men. *British journal of addiction*, **87**: 891–900 (1992).

94. BABOR, T.F. & GRANT, M., ED. *Project on identification and management of alcohol-related problems. Report on phase II: a randomized clinical trial of brief interventions in primary health care*. Geneva, World Health Organization, 1992 (document WHO/PSA/91.5).

95. SCOTT, E. & ANDERSON, P. Randomized controlled trial of general practitioner intervention in women with excessive alcohol consumption. *Drug and alcohol review*, **10**: 313–321 (1991).

96. SONG, F. ET AL. Can brief interventions reduce alcohol consumption in drinkers at risk of alcohol-related harm? A meta-analysis of clinical trials. *Addiction* (in press).

97. HEATHER, N. Interpreting the evidence on brief interventions; the need for caution. *Alcohol and alcoholism*, **30**: 287–296 (1995).

98. SANCHEZ-CRAIG, M. ET AL. Theory and methods for secondary prevention of alcohol problems: a cognitively-based approach. *In:* Cox, W.M., ed. *Treatment and prevention of alcohol problems: a resource manual.* New York, Academic Press, 1987.
99. ZWEBEN, A. ET AL. A comparison of brief advice and conjoint therapy in the treatment of alcohol abuse: the results of the Marital Systems study. *British journal of addiction*, **83**: 899–916 (1988).
100. MILLER, W.R. & MUNOZ, R.F. *How to control your drinking.* Albuquerque, NM, University of New Mexico Press, 1982.
101. ROBERTSON, I. & HEATHER, N. *Let's drink to your health!* Leicester, British Psychological Society, 1985.
102. RICHMOND, R.L. ET AL. Controlled evaluation of a general practice-based brief intervention for excessive drinking. *Addiction*, **90**: 119–132 (1995).
103. KRISTENSON, H. ET AL. Identification and intervention of heavy drinking in middle-aged men: results and follow-up of 24:60 months of long-term study with randomized controls. *Alcoholism: clinical and experimental research,* **20**: 203–209 (1983).
104. MCINTOSH, I.D. Alcohol-related disabilities in general hospital patients: a critical review of the evidence. *International journal of the addictions*, **17**: 609–639 (1982).
105. CHICK, J. ET AL. Counselling problem drinkers in medical wards: a controlled study. *British medical journal*, **83**: 159–170 (1985).
106. DICLEMENTE, C.C. ET AL. The process of smoking cessation: an analysis of the precontemplation, contemplation and preparation stages of change. *Journal of consulting and clinical psychology*, **59**: 295–304 (1991).
107. PROCHASKA, J.O. & DICLEMENTE, C.C. Stages of change in the modification or problem behaviors. *In:* Hersen, M. et al., ed. *Progress in behavior modification.* Newbury Park, CA, Sage, 1992.
108. PROCHASKA, J.O. ET AL. In search of how people change: applications to addictive behaviors. *American psychologist*, **47**: 1102–1114 (1992).
109. DAVIDSON, R. ET AL., ED. *Counselling problem drinkers.* London, Tavistock/Routledge, 1991.
110. ORFORD, J. *Excessive appetites: a psychological view of addictions.* London, John Wiley & Sons, 1985.

111. *Alcoholics Anonymous.* New York, Alcoholics Anonymous World Services, 1980.
112. MILLER, W.R. ET AL. Enhancing motivation for change in problem drinking: a controlled comparison of two therapist styles. *Journal of consulting and clinical psychology*, **61**: 455–461 (1993).
113. ROGERS, C.R. *Client-centred therapy.* Cambridge, MA, Riverside Press, 1951.
114. MILLER, W.R. ET AL. Motivational interviewing with problem drinkers, II. The drinker's check-up as a preventive intervention. *Behavioral psychotherapy*, **16**: 251–268 (1988).
115. MILLER, W.R. ET AL. *Motivational enhancement therapy manual.* Washington, DC, National Institute on Alcohol Abuse and Alcoholism, 1992 (Project MATCH Monograph Series, Vol. 2).
116. ROLLNICK, S. ET AL. Negotiating behaviour change in medical settings: the development of brief motivational interviewing. *Journal of mental health*, **1**: 25–37 (1992).
117. BROWN, J.M. & MILLER, W.R. Impact of motivational interviewing on participation and outcome in residential alcoholism treatment. *Psychology of addictive behaviors*, **7**: 211–218 (1993).
118. ROGERS, C.R. The necessary and sufficient conditions for therapeutic personality change. *Journal of consulting psychology*, **21**: 95–103 (1957).
119. TRUAX, C.B. & CARKHUFF, R.R. *Toward effective counselling and psychotherapy.* Chicago, Aldine, 1967.
120. FULLER, R.K. Antidipsotropic medications. *In:* Hester, R.K. & Miller, W.R., ed. *Handbook of alcoholism treatment approaches: effective alternatives.* New York, Pergamon. 1989.
121. BREWER, C. Probation-linked treatment with disulfiram: dosage and the alcohol–disulfiram challenge. *In:* Brewer, C., ed. *Treatment options in addiction: medical management of alcohol and opiate abuse.* London, Gaskell, 1993.
122. BREWER, C. How effective is the standard dose of disulfiram? A review of the ethanol–disulfiram reaction in practice. *British journal of psychiatry*, **144**: 200–202 (1984).
123. FULLER, R.K. & ROTH, H.P. Disulfiram for the treatment of alcoholism: an evaluation in 128 men. *Annals of internal medicine*, **90**: 901–904 (1979).

124. FULLER, R.K. & WILLIFORD, W.O. Life-table analysis of abstinence in a study evaluating the efficacy of disulfiram. *Alcoholism: clinical and experimental research*, **4**: 298–301 (1980).

125. FULLER, R.K. ET AL. Disulfiram treatment of alcoholism: a Veterans Administration co-operative study. *Journal of the American Medical Association*, **256**: 1449–1455 (1986).

126. HEATHER, N. Disulfiram treatment for alcoholism: deserves re-examination. *British medical journal*, **299**: 471–472 (1989).

127. HEATHER, N. Disulfiram treatment for alcohol problems: is it effective and, if so, why? *In:* Brewer, C., ed. *Treatment options in addiction: medical management of alcohol and opiate abuse.* London, Gaskell, 1993.

128. AZRIN, N.H. ET AL. Alcoholism treatment by disulfiram and community reinforcement therapy. *Journal of behavior therapy and experimental psychiatry*, **13**: 105–112 (1982).

129. CHICK, J. ET AL. Disulfiram treatment of alcoholism. *British journal of psychiatry*, **161**: 84–89 (1992).

130. JOHNSEN, J. ET AL. A double-blind placebo controlled study of male alcoholics given a subcutaneous disulfiram implantation. *British journal of addiction*, **82**: 607–613 (1987).

131. BREWER, C. The management of opiate abuse: learning from other addictions. *Journal of drug issues*, **18**: 679–697 (1988).

132. PEACHEY, J.E. ET AL. Calcium carbimide in alcoholism treatment. Part 1: a placebo-controlled double-blind clinical trial of short-term efficacy. *British journal of addiction*, **84**: 877–887 (1989).

133. VOLPICELLI, J.R. ET AL. Naltrexone and the treatment of alcohol dependence: initial observations. *In:* Reid, L.B., ed. *Opioids, bulimia, alcohol abuse and alcoholism.* New York, Springer-Verlag, 1990.

134. O'MALLEY, S.S. ET AL. Naltrexone and coping skills therapy for alcohol dependence. *Archives of general psychiatry*, **49**: 881–887 (1992).

135. SELLERS, E.M. ET AL. Opportunities for treatment of psychoactive substance use disorders with serotonergic medications. *Journal of clinical psychiatry*, **52**: 49–54 (1991).

136. LITTEN, R.Z. & ALLEN, J.P. Pharmacotherapies for alcoholism: promising agents and clinical issues. *Alcoholism: clinical and experimental research*, **15**: 620–633 (1991).

137. AMIT, Z. ET AL. Serotonin uptake inhibitors: effects on motivated consummatory behaviours. *Journal of clinical psychiatry*, **12**: 55–60 (1991).

138. NARANJO, C.A. ET AL. Effects of citalopram and a brief psycho-social intervention on alcohol intake, dependence and problems. *Addiction*, **90**: 87–99 (1995).

139. BORG, V. Bromocriptine in the prevention of alcohol abuse. *Acta psychiatrica scandinavica*, **68**: 100–110 (1983).

140. SHAW, G.K. ET AL. Tiapride in the prevention of relapse in recently detoxified alcoholics. *British journal of psychiatry*, **165**: 515–523 (1994).

141. LHUINTRE, J.P. ET AL. Ability of calcium bis acetyl homotaurine, a GABA agonist, to prevent relapse in weaned alcoholics. *Lancet*, **1**: 1014–1016 (1985).

142. SAMSON, H.H. ET AL. Oral ethanol reinforcement in the rat: effect of the partial inverse benzodiazepine agonist RO 15-4513. *Pharmacology, biochemistry and behavior*, **27**: 517–519 (1987).

143. LHUINTRE, J.P. ET AL. Acamprosate appears to decrease alcohol intake in weaned alcoholics. *Alcohol and alcoholism*, **25**: 613–622 (1990).

144. FAWCETT, J. ET AL. A double-blind, placebo-controlled trial of lithium carbonate therapy for alcoholism. *Archives of general psychiatry*, **44**: 248–256 (1987).

145. TOLLEFSON, G. ET AL. Treatment of comorbid generalized anxiety in a recently detoxified alcoholic population. *Journal of clinical psychopharmacology*, **12**: 19–26 (1992)

146. BANDURA, A. *Social foundations of thought and action: a social cognitive theory.* Englewood Cliffs, NJ, Prentice-Hall, 1986.

147. LAUNDERGAN, J.C. & WILLIAMS, T. The Hazelden Residential Family Program: a combined systems and disease model approach. *In:* O'Farrell, T. J., ed. *Treating alcohol problems: marital and family interventions.* New York, Guilford, 1993.

148. MCCRADY, B.S. ET AL. Effects of joint hospital admission and couples treatment for hospitalized alcoholics: a pilot study. *Addictive behaviors*, **4**: 155–165 (1979).

149. O'FARRELL, T.J. A behavioural marital therapy couples group program for alcoholics and their spouses. *In:* O'Farrell, T.J., ed. *Treating alcohol problems: marital and family interventions.* New York, Guilford, 1993.
150. NOEL, N.E. & MCCRADY, B.S. Alcohol-focused spouse involvement with behavioral marital therapy. *In:* O'Farrell, T.J., ed. *Treating alcohol problems: marital and family interventions.* New York, Guilford, 1993.
151. MCCRADY, B. ET AL. Comparative effectiveness of three types of spouse involvement in outpatient behavioral alcoholism treatment. *Journal of studies on alcohol*, **47**: 459–476 (1986).
152. MCCRADY, B. ET AL. Comparative effectiveness of three types of spouse-involved alcohol treatment: outcome 18 months after treatment. *British journal of addiction*, **86**: 1415–1424 (1991).
153. O'FARRELL, T.J. ET AL. Evaluating behavioral marital therapy for male alcoholics: effects on marital adjustment and communication from before to after therapy. *Behavior therapy*, **16**: 147–167 (1985).
154. O'FARRELL, T.J. ET AL. Behavioral marital therapy for male alcoholics: marital and drinking adjustment during the two years after treatment. *Behavior therapy*, **23**: 529–549 (1992).
155. BOWERS, T.G. & AL-REHDA, M.R. A comparison of outcome with group/marital and standard/individual therapies with alcoholics. *Journal of studies on alcohol*, **51**: 301–309 (1990).
156. O'FARRELL, T.J. & COWLES, K.S. Marital and family therapy. *In:* Hester, R.K. & Miller, W.R., ed. *Handbook of alcoholism treatment approaches: effective alternatives.* New York, Pergamon, 1989.
157. MCCRADY, B.S. The family in the change process. *In:* Miller, W.R. & Heather, N., ed. *Treating addictive behaviors: processes of change.* New York, Plenum, 1986.
158. NOEL, N. ET AL. Predictors of attrition from an outpatient alcoholism couples treatment program. *Journal of studies on alcohol*, **48**: 229–235 (1987).
159. SISSON, R.W. & AZRIN, N.H. Family-member involvement to initiate and promote treatment of problem drinkers. *Journal of behavior therapy and experimental psychiatry*, **17**: 15–21 (1986).

160. SISSON, R.W. & AZRIN, N.H. Community reinforcement training for families: a method to get alcoholics into treatment. *In:* O'Farrell, T. J., ed. *Treating alcohol problems: marital and family interventions.* New York, Guilford, 1993.
161. HUNT, G.M. & AZRIN, N.H. A community-reinforcement approach to alcoholism. *Behaviour research and therapy*, **11**: 91–104 (1973).
162. SISSON, R.W. & AZRIN, N.H. The community reinforcement approach. *In:* Hester, R.K. & Miller, W.R., ed. *Handbook of alcoholism treatment approaches: effective alternatives.* New York, Pergamon, 1989.
163. AZRIN, N.H. Improvements in the community-reinforcement approach to alcoholism. *Behavior research and therapy*, **14**: 339–348 (1976).
164. MALLAMS, J.H. ET AL. A social-systems approach to resocializing alcoholics in the community. *Journal of studies on alcohol*, **43**: 1115–1123 (1982).
165. STOCKWELL, T. & TOWN, C. Anxiety and stress management. *In:* Hester, R.K. & Miller, W.R., ed. *Handbook of alcoholism treatment approaches: effective alternatives.* New York, Pergamon, 1989.
166. ROSENBERG, S.D. *Relaxation training and a differential assessment of alcoholism.* Dissertation, California School of Professional Psychology, San Diego, CA, 1979.
167. LANYON, R.I. ET AL. An aversion desensitization treatment for alcoholism. *Journal of consulting and clinical psychology*, **38**: 394–398 (1972).
168. HEDBERG, A.G. & CAMPBELL, L.M. A comparison of four behavioral treatment approaches to alcoholism. *Journal of behavior therapy and experimental psychiatry*, **5**: 251–256 (1974).
169. BECK, A.T. ET AL. *Cognitive therapy of depression.* New York, Guilford, 1979.
170. ELLIS, A. ET AL. *Rational-emotive therapy with alcoholics and substance abusers.* New York, Pergamon, 1988.
171. ELLIS, A. & HARPER, R.A. *A new guide to rational living.* North Hollywood, CA, Wilshire, 1975.
172. MEICHEMBAUM, D. *Cognitive-behavior modification: an integrative approach.* New York, Plenum, 1977.

173. JACKSON, P. & OEI, T.P.S. Social skills training and cognitive restructuring with alcoholics. *Drug and alcohol dependence*, **3**: 369–374 (1978).

174. OEI, T.P.S. & JACKSON, P.R. Social skills and cognitive behavioural approaches to the treatment of problem drinking. *Journal of studies on alcohol*, **43**: 532–547 (1982).

175. BRANDSMA, J.M. ET AL. *Outpatient treatment of alcoholism: a review and comparative study*. Baltimore, MD, University Park Press, 1980.

176. ABRAMS, D.B. & NIAURA, R.S. Social learning theory of alcohol use and abuse. *In:* Blane, H. & Leonard, K., ed. *Psychological theories of drinking and alcoholism.* New York, Guilford, 1987.

177. CHANEY, E.F. Social skills training. *In:* Hester, R.K. & Miller, W.R., ed. *Handbook of alcoholism treatment approaches: effective alternatives.* New York, Pergamon, 1989.

178. JONES, S.L. ET AL. Skill training with alcoholics: a clinical extension. *Addictive behaviors*, **7**: 285–290 (1982).

179. OEI, T.P.S. & JACKSON, P. Long-term effects of groups and individual social skills training with alcoholics. *Addictive behaviors*, **5**: 129–136 (1980).

180. FERRELL, W.L. & GALASSI, J.P. Assertion training and human relations training in the treatment of chronic alcoholics. *International journal of the addictions*, **16**: 959–968 (1981).

181. MONTI, P.M. ET AL. Communication skills training: communication skills training with family and cognitive behavioral mood management training for alcoholics. *Journal of studies on alcohol*, **51**: 263–270 (1990).

182. D'ZURILLA, T.J. & GOLDFRIED, M.R. Problem solving and behavior modification. *Journal of abnormal psychology*, **78**: 107–126 (1971).

183. SANCHEZ-CRAIG, M. & WALKER, K. Teaching coping skills to chronic alcoholics in a coeducational halfway house, I. Assessment of programme effects. *British journal of addiction*, **77**: 35–50 (1982).

184. COONEY, N.L. ET AL. Matching alcoholics to coping skills or interactional therapies: two-year follow-up results. *Journal of consulting and clinical psychology*, **59**: 598–601 (1991).

185. HESTER, R.K. & MILLER, W.R. Self-control training. *In:* Hester, R.K. & Miller, W.R., ed. *Handbook of alcoholism treatment approaches: effective alternatives.* New York, Pergamon, 1989.
186. SANCHEZ-CRAIG, M. ET AL. Random assignment to abstinence and controlled drinking: evaluation of a cognitive–behavioural program for problem drinkers. *Journal of consulting and clinical psychology*, **52**: 390–403 (1984).
187. SANCHEZ-CRAIG, M. & LEI, H. Disadvantages of imposing the goal of abstinence on problem drinkers: an empirical study. *British journal of addiction*, **81**: 505–512 (1986).
188. MILLER, W.R. & BACA, L.M. Two-year follow-up of bibliotherapy and therapist-directed controlled drinking training for problem drinkers. *Behavior therapy*, **14**: 441–448 (1983).
189. RIMMELE, C.T. ET AL. Aversion therapies. *In:* Hester, R.K. & Miller, W.R., ed. *Handbook of alcoholism treatment approaches: effective alternatives.* New York, Pergamon, 1989.
190. MALETZKY, B.M. Assisted covert sensitization for drug abuse. *International journal of the addictions*, **9**: 411–429 (1974).
191. ELKINS, R.L. Covert sensitization and alcoholism: contributions of successful conditioning to subsequent abstinence maintenance. *Addictive behaviors*, **5**: 67–89 (1980).
192. HEATHER, N. & GREELEY, J. Cue exposure in the treatment of drug dependence: the potential of a new method for preventing relapse. *Drug and alcohol review*, **9**: 155–168 (1990).
193. DRUMMOND, D.C. ET AL. *Addictive behaviour: cue exposure theory and practice.* Chichester, John Wiley & Sons, 1995.
194. WILSON, G.T. Cognitive processes in addiction. *British journal of addiction*, **82**: 343–353 (1987).
195. BLAKEY, R. & BAKER, R. An exposure approach to alcohol abuse. *Behaviour research and therapy*, **18**: 319–325 (1980).
196. HEATHER, N. ET AL. Alcohol cue exposure directed at a goal of moderate drinking. *Journal of behavior therapy and experimental psychiatry*, **24**: 187–195 (1993).
197. KADDEN, R. ET AL. *Cognitive–behavioral coping skills therapy manual.* Washington, DC, National Institute on Alcohol Abuse and Alcoholism, 1992 (Project MATCH Monograph Series, Vol. 3).

198. HODGSON, R.J. & RANKIN, H.J. Modification of excessive drinking by cue exposure. *Behaviour research and therapy*, **14**: 305–307 (1976).
199. MONTI, P.M. ET AL. Cue exposure with coping skills treatment for male alcoholics: a preliminary investigation. *Journal of consulting and clinical psychology*, **61**: 1011–1019 (1993).
200. DRUMMOND, D.C. & GLAUTIER, S. A controlled trial of cue exposure treatment in alcohol dependence. *Journal of consulting and clinical psychology*, **62**: 809–817 (1994).
201. BANDURA, A. *Social learning theory.* Englewood Cliffs, NJ, Prentice-Hall, 1976.
202. ANNIS, H.M. & DAVIS, C.S. Relapse prevention. *In:* Hester, R.K. & Miller, W.R., ed. *Handbook of alcoholism treatment approaches: effective alternatives.* New York, Pergamon, 1989.
203. CUMMINGS, C. ET AL. Relapse: strategies of prevention and prediction. *In:* Miller, W.R., ed. *The addictive behaviours.* Oxford, Pergamon, 1980.
204. SAUNDERS, B. & ALLSOP, S. Relapse: a psychological perspective. *British journal of addiction*, **82**: 417–429 (1987).
205. HEATHER, N. & STALLARD, A. Does the Marlatt model underestimate the importance of conditioned craving in the relapse process? *In:* Gossop, M., ed. *Relapse and addictive behaviour.* London, Tavistock/Routledge, 1989.
206. MARLATT, G.A. Cue exposure and relapse prevention in the treatment of addictive behaviors. *Addictive behaviors*, **15**: 395–399 (1990).
207. MCCRADY, B.S. Relapse prevention: a couples-therapy perspective. *In:* O'Farrell, T.J., ed. *Treating alcohol problems, marital and family interventions.* New York, Guilford, 1993.
208. ITO, J.R. & DONOVAN, D.M. Aftercare in alcoholism treatment: a review. *In:* Miller, W.R. & Heather, N., ed. *Treating addictive behaviors: processes of change.* New York, Plenum, 1986.
209. MOOS, R.H. ET AL. *Alcoholism treatment: context, process and outcome.* New York, Oxford University Press, 1990.
210. O'FARRELL, T.J. Couples relapse prevention sessions after a behavioral marital therapy couples group program. *In:* O'Farrell, T.J., ed. *Treating alcohol problems: marital and family interventions.* New York, Guilford, 1993.

211. OSSIP-KLEIN, D.J. & RYCHTARIK, R.G. Behavioral contracts between alcoholics and family members: improving aftercare participation and maintaining sobriety after inpatient alcoholism treatment. *In:* O'Farrell, T.J., ed. *Treating alcohol problems: marital and family interventions.* New York, Guilford, 1993.

212. AHLES, T.A. ET AL. Impact of aftercare arrangements on the maintenance of treatment success in abusive drinkers. *Addictive behaviors*, **8**: 53–58 (1983).

213. O'FARRELL, T.J. ET AL. Behavioural marital therapy with and without additional couples relapse prevention sessions for alcoholics and their wives. *Journal of studies on alcohol*, **54**: 652–666 (1993).

214. MAKELA, K. Social and cultural preconditions of Alcoholics Anonymous (AA) and factors associated with the strength of AA. *British journal of addiction*, **86**: 1405–1413 (1991).

215. ROBINSON, D. *Talking out of alcoholism: the self-help process of Alcoholics Anonymous*. London, Croom Helm, 1979.

216. MCCRADY, B.S. & IRVINE, S. Self-help groups. *In:* Hester, R.K. & Miller, W.R., ed. *Handbook of alcoholism treatment approaches: effective alternatives.* New York, Pergamon, 1989.

217. DITMAN, K.S. ET AL. A controlled experiment on the use of court probation for drunk arrests. *American journal of psychiatry*, **124**: 160–163 (1967).

218. MCCRADY, B.S. & MILLER, W.R. *Research on Alcoholics Anonymous: opportunities and alternatives.* New Brunswick, NJ, Rutgers Center of Alcohol Studies, 1993.

219. EMRICK, C.D. Alcoholics Anonymous: affiliation processes and effectiveness as treatment. *Alcoholism: clinical and experimental research*, **11**: 416–423 (1987).

220. OGBORNE, A.C. & GLASER, F.B. Characteristics of affiliates of Alcoholics Anonymous: a review of the literature. *Journal of studies on alcohol*, **42**: 661–675 (1981).

221. DAVIES, D.L. Stabilized addiction and normal drinking in recovered alcohol addicts. *In:* Steinberg, H., ed. *Scientific basis of drug dependence.* London, Churchill Livingstone, 1969.

222. RUZEK, J. The Drinkwatchers experience: a description and progress report on services for controlled drinkers. *In:* Stockwell, T. & Clement, S., ed. *Helping the problem drinker: new initiatives in community care.* London, Croom Helm, 1987.
223. VELTEN, E. Trends in the lay treatment of addictions. *Annual review of addictions research and treatment*, **3**: 199–220 (1994).
224. PEELE, S. *Diseasing of America: addiction treatment out of control.* Boston, Houghton Mifflin, 1989.
225. COOK, C.H. The Minnesota model in the management of drug and alcohol dependency: miracle, method or myth? Part I. The philosophy and the programme. *British journal of addiction*, **83**: 625–634 (1988).
226. KESO, L. & SALASPURO, M. Inpatient treatment of employed alcoholics: a randomized clinical trial of Hazelden-type and traditional treatment. *Alcoholism: clinical and experimental research*, **14**: 584–589 (1990).
227. HOWARD, M.O. Assessing the cost–effectiveness of alcoholism treatments: a comment on Holder, Longabaugh, Miller and Rubonis. *Journal of studies on alcohol*, **54**: 667–674 (1993).
228. HOLDER, H.E. & HALLAN, J.B. Impact of alcoholism treatment on total health care costs: a six year study. *Advances in alcohol and substance abuse*, **6**: 1–15 (1986).
229. JONES, K.R. & VISCHI, T.R. Impact of alcohol, drug abuse and mental health treatment on medical care utilization. *Medical care*, **17**: 1–82 (1979).
230. SAXE, L. ET AL. *The effectiveness and costs of alcoholism treatment.* Washington, DC, US Government Printing Office, 1983 (Congress of the United States Office of Technology Assessment, Health Technology Case Study 22).
231. HOLDER, H.D. Alcoholism treatment and potential health care cost saving. *Medical care*, **25**: 52–71 (1987).
232. LUCKEY, J.W. Justifying alcohol treatment on the basis of cost savings: the “offset” literature. *Alcohol health and research world*, **12**: 8–15 (1987).
233. GREENSTREET, R.L. *Cost-effective alternatives in alcoholism treatment.* Springfield, IL, Charles C. Thomas, 1988.

234. MILLER, W.R. & TAYLOR, C.A. Relative effectiveness of bibliotherapy, individual and group self-control training in the treatment of problem drinkers. *Addictive behaviors*, **5**: 13–24 (1980).
235. LONGABAUGH, R. ET AL. Cost-effectiveness of alcoholism treatment in partial vs. inpatient settings: six month outcomes. *Journal of studies on alcohol*, **44**: 1049–1071 (1983).
236. MCLACHLAN, J.F.C. & STEIN, R.L. Evaluation of a day clinic for alcoholics. *Journal of studies on alcohol*, **43**: 261–272 (1982).
237. MCLELLAN, A.T. ET AL. Is treatment for substance abuse effective? *Journal of the American Medical Association*, **247**: 1423–1428 (1982).
238. WANBERG, K.W.J. ET AL. Hospital versus community treatment of alcoholism problems. *International journal of mental health*, **3**: 160–176 (1974).
239. TOLLEY, K. & ROWLAND, N. Identification of alcohol-related problems in a general hospital setting: a cost–effectiveness evaluation. *British journal of addiction*, **86**: 429–438 (1991).
240. ROOM, R. Treatment-seeking populations and larger realities. *In*: Edwards, G. & Grant, M., ed. *Alcoholism treatment in transition*. London, Croom Helm, 1980.
241. FILLMORE, K.M. & KELSO, D. Coercion into alcoholism treatment: meanings for the disease concept of alcoholism. *Journal of drug issues*, **17**: 301–319 (1987).
242. WEISNER, C.M. Coercion into alcohol treatment. Appendix D. *In*: Institute of Medicine. *Broadening the base of treatment for alcohol problems*. Washington, DC, US Government Printing Office, 1990.
243. SZASZ, T.S. *The myth of mental illness: foundations of a theory of personal conduct*. New York, Hoeber-Harper, 1961.
244. SZASZ, T.S. *Law, liberty and psychiatry: an inquiry into the social uses of mental health practices*. New York, Macmillan, 1963.
245. SZASZ, T.S. *Ceremonial chemistry: the ritual persecution of drugs, addicts and pushers*. London, Routledge & Kegan Paul, 1975.
246. FINGARETTE, H. *Heavy drinking: the myth of alcoholism as a disease*. Berkeley, CA, University of California Press, 1988.

247. FINGARETTE, H. The perils of Powell: in search of a factual foundation for "the disease concept of alcoholism". *Harvard law review*, **83**: 793–807 (1970).

248. CONRAD, P. & SCHNEIDER, J.W. *Deviance and medicalization: from badness to sickness.* St Louis, MO, C.V. Mosley, 1980.

249. FINN, P. Decriminalization of public drunkenness: response of the health care system. *Journal of studies on alcohol*, **46**: 7–23 (1985).

250. TRICE, H. & BEYER, J. Social control in worksettings: using the constructive confrontation strategy with problem-drinking employees. *Journal of drug issues*, **12**: 21–49 (1982).

251. ROSS, H.L. *Deterring the drinking driver: legal policy and social control.* Lexington, MA, Lexington Books, 1984.

252. TAYLOR, I. ET AL. *The new criminology: for a social theory of deviance.* London, Routledge, 1973.

253. KAELBER, C. & NOBEL, J. *Procedures for assessing alcohol treatment needs.* Rockville, MD, National Institute on Alcohol Abuse and Alcoholism, 1982.

254. RUSH, B. A systems approach to estimating the required capacity of alcohol treatment services. *British journal of addiction*, **85**: 49–59 (1990).

255. GODFREY, C. ET AL. *Assessing needs for alcohol services: guidance for purchasers. Report to the Department of Health.* York, Centre for Health Economics, University of York, 1993.

256. EDWARDS, G. & UNNITHAL, S. *Alcohol misuse.* London, National Health Service Management Executive, 1992 (Epidemiologically-based Needs Assessment Report, No. 7).

257. OGBORNE, A.C. & RUSH, B.R. Specialized addictions assessment/referral services in Ontario: a review of their characteristics and roles in the addiction treatment system. *British journal of addiction*, **85**: 197–204 (1990).

258. SOBELL, M.B. & SOBELL, L.C. Controlled drinking after 25 years: how important was the great debate? *Addiction*, **90**: 1149–1153 (1995).

259. COPELAND, J. & HALL, W. A comparison of predictors of treatment drop-out of women seeking drug and alcohol treatment in a specialist women's and two traditional mixed-sex treatment services. *British journal of addiction*, **87**: 883–890 (1992).

260. ROLLNICK, S. ET AL. Methods of helping patients with behaviour change. *British medical journal*, **307**: 188–190 (1993).
261. TETHER, P. & ROBINSON, D. *Preventing alcohol problems: a guide to local action*. London, Tavistock, 1986.
262. MCINTOSH, I.D. Alcohol-related disabilities in general hospital. *International journal of the addictions*, **17**: 609–639 (1982).